Inhabitants
of
Baltimore County
Maryland

1692-1763

F. Edward Wright

WILLOW BEND BOOKS
2007

WILLOW BEND BOOKS
AN IMPRINT OF HERITAGE BOOKS, INC.

Books, CDs, and more—Worldwide

For our listing of thousands of titles see our website
at
www.HeritageBooks.com

Published 2007 by
HERITAGE BOOKS, INC.
Publishing Division
65 East Main Street
Westminster, Maryland 21157-5026

International Standard Book Number: 978-1-58549-010-5

CONTENTS

Inhabitants of Baltimore County, 1692 - 1763

Introduction

Genealogists have long known that very few of our forebears left wills, and indeed many of them did not own land, attend a church regularly, or leave any estate worth adminstering. They often moved from place to place before settling down. For those perpatetic individuals whose lives and activities are not mentioned in church, probate, or land records, it may be only the recording of their name in an "occasional" list that places in a specific locality at a precise time. Thus Frederick Hopkins, listed as a taxable in the household of Richard King Stevenson in the 1737 tax list of Patapsco Lower Hundred, may not have had his marriage recorded in any extant church records, may not have left an estate in Baltimore County, or owned land, and may have moved elsewhere, but the inclusion of his name on this tax list established that he was in Baltimore County at that time, and that he was 16 years or older, and that he was living in someone else's household, either as an indentured servant or perhaps as a relative.

Lists not only place an individual in a certian place and time, but they may shed light on his life styles, philosophies, political beliefs, or socio-econonic status. The 1737 Levy Papers show that John Carpenter was allowed L 1.10.0 for maintaining Prudence Cox and an orphan child for three months, while William Amoss was allowed L 1.1.4 for bringing in 107 squirrels' heads. One wonders if William Amos was a crack marksman or whether the total represents the number of squirrels bagged by himself, members of the family, and servants.

The lists in this volume were gathered from a variety of sources, and the compilation of the material was made easier by the work of a number of genealogists, antiquarians, and indexers. The tax lists for 1692, 1694, 1695, and 1737, and the levy papers were originally discovered by William N. Wilkins in the Baltimore County Court Proceedings and the papers at the Maryland Historical Society. He transcribed them, typed them, and indexed them, and put copies of his work in the Maryland Historical Society and the Enoch Pratt Free Library. Some of the tax lists for Baltimore County, for the years 1699 through 1706, have been published by Raymond B. Clark, Jr., and Sara Seth Clark. Mr. Wilkins may be best known for his monumental card file at the Maryland Histroical Society. It is an invaluable finding aid for material buried in the otherwise unindexed genealogical collections and local and county histories used by hundreds of genealogists.

The Reverend Mr. Ethan Allen was a clergyman of the Protestant Episcopal Church who gathered a great deal of material on the history of Episcopal parishes in Maryland. His work has unearthed the names of contributors and vestrymen and wardens of St. Thomas' Parish, and the vestrymen, wardens, and bachelors taxed in St. Paul's Parish.

A number of petitions (e.g., the 1750 petition to resurvey Baltimore Town, and the 1755 petition to repair St. Paul's Church), the levy papers of 1739, and the 1760 list of Quakers who contributed to the sufferers of the Bosotn fire, were all published in the Calendar of Maryland State Papers:

Inhabitants of Baltimore County, 1692 - 1763

The Black Books, and are taken from the original papers on deposit at the Maryland State Archives in Annapolis.

Several petitions were found in the Baltimore County Court Proceedings by the late William Bose Marye, and cited in his many articles on the roads, mills, and place names of Baltimore and Harford Counties. These articles, published in the Maryland Historical Magazine, span the years from 1915 to 1964. Mr. Marye's collection of notebooks and folders were left to the Maryland Historical Society, and can be seen in the Manuscript Division.

Dr. Richard B. Miller, of Pasadena, California, spent years researching Maryland families and abstracting a variety of sources. Many of his papers were sent to the Maryland Historical Society and many were sent to the Baltimore County Genealogical Society. Among his papers were two notebooks of abstracts of Baltimore County land records covering the years 1659 through 1746. The land record books contain not only deeds of conveyance and leases, but lists of cattle and hog marks, convicts brought into Maryland, alienation fees, and debtors. These lists have been abstracted and included in this volume.

Finally a number of documents have been extracted by the compiler of this volume from original records at the Maryland Historical Society and the Maryland State Archives. Some of these include the Assessor's Field Book of 1750 and the Baltimore County Debt Book of 1754.

Because these lists were originally compiled for specific purposes, they exhibit a variety of characteristics. The tax lists listed all white males 16 years of age and older, and all slaves of either sex, of whatever age. White women were usually only named when they were widows, and the servants and/or slaves at their plantations were being enumerated. The levy papers and levy lists contain names of individuals who were compensated by the county government for a variety of services, ranging from caring for an indigent pensioner to bringing in squireels' or wolves' heads for a bounty. These services reveal much about the daily activities of early inhabitants of the county. Lists of contributors to the building of St. Thomas' Church, or to the sufferers of the Boston fire reveal the religious affiliation of those named as well as indicate that they were willing to contribute to what they deemed a worthy cause. The lists of cattle and hog marks registered by a number of people not only place those individuals in the county, but may point the way to establishing possible relationships. It has been suggested that these livestock marks, forerunners of the cattle brands of the American West, may be considered a form of American heraldry since they were visual symbols used to identify property, and may have been handed down (with some variations) from father to his sons.

Two categories of lists contain direct genealogical information. The leases for three lifetimes usually contain the name of the lessee, his or her age, and the names and ages of two other family members. Often the youngest child of the lessee was named so that the lease would run for the longest possible time. The French and Indian War saw the enactment of a law by the Assembly of Maryland stipulating that the vestries of the various parishes were to compile annual lists of bachelors over the age of 25 whose net worth was 100 pounds or more, and those whose net worth was 300 pounds or more, and that these bachelors were to pay a special tax to help finance the war.

It is hoped that persons using these lists will be able to locate individuals not previously known to have lived in the county, and to gain a deeper insight into the lives activies of early county residents. In addition researchers will have gained a better idea of the variety of types of records that can be found in unlikely places.

Robert Barnes

BALTIMORE COUNTY TAX LIST - 1692

Taken from Baltimore County Court Proceedings, Liber F, No. 1, folio 225-229, 1691-1693. Held by State Archives, Annapolis, Maryland. Arranged by William N. Wilkins.

A List of taxables taken by Richard Guin - Constable of the South Side of Patapscoe River July the Fifteenth 1692.

Thomas Homewood, Richard Steere /2
Thomas Knightsmith /1
William Hawkins, Randall Jones, Stephen White /3
Sam Smith, James Smith /2
John Smith /1
Robert Alling /1
Richard Guin, John Herin, Ralph Barrow, William Darte (Darfe) /4
Richard Robinson /1
Henry Chappell /1
John Looket, Joseph Tolson /2
James Jackson /1
Edw. Tessell /1
John Bass, Benjamin Gargall, Henry Fusse and 3 slaves /6
Philip Roper, Will Seger /2
John Stevens, Will Stevens /2
Henry Hall /1
William Slade, Jno Munfeild /2
Christopher Cockey /1
Isaack Jackson /1
James Murrey, Jno. Scott, Jonathan Heel, 3 slaves /6
Tho. Hooker, James Harlem, Jonas Williams /3
Will: Hicks, Jno Clarke /2
Tho: Hammond, Edward Scott, Isaack Majerd, 3 slaves, 1 denied /6
Will: Budd /1
Geo. Norman, a man denied named Josias /2
Stephen Hant /1
Edward Cockey /1
Richard Cromwell, Robert Forgasin, Henry Weyatt, John Marsh, Tho: Cansell, Jno. Egleston, 1 slave, and 1 more denied /7
George Ashman, Rich'd. Pearle, Henry Butler, Rich'd. Russell, John Bone, Christopher Perdue, John Gosses, and 3 slaves /10
Wm. Hicks (none shown)

Joseph Williams, Jno. Beckham, Symon Feno, Charles Billum, Mermaduke Thompson /5

A list of taxables taken of the Northside of Patapscoe Hundred as given under my hand and seal this present year 1692 - Nicholas Corbin, Constable of Patapscoe Hundred.

Joseph Heathcole, Hector McLane, August Moone, 2 negro slaves, 1 called Solan, the other Betty /5
John Harriman /1
Laurance Yoston /1
Rich'd Tomson /1
Rich'd Sampson, Isaack Sampson, Martin Taylor, Jno. Riston /4
Nicholas Power /1
Rob't Tailler /1
Edmund Baxter, Jno. Lekens /2
Jno. Hardin, Joseph Strawbridge, Michaell Young, John Wells /4
Sam'll Greenwood, Tho. Bell /2
Will Wilkinson, Rich'd Sadd, Jno Chase, Christopher Bumbridge, Tho. Jushman /5
Jno Rows, Jno Lovell /2
Edw'd Mumford, Joseph Peregoe /2
Tho. Durbin /1
Will Fenton /1
Robert Wilmuth, Jno Wilmuth /2
Thomas Roberts, William Frame /2
Moses Edwards /1
Daniell Ellerd /1
Micha. Rutley /1
Andrew Anderson, Tho. Hancock /2
Christopher Shaw, Ambrose Hogge /2
Launcellot Pulley /1
Will Farfare /1
Francis Watkins, Mich: Gormagonscott, Edwd. Cantwell, Edmond Moore /4
Robt. Gardner /1
Humphry Day /1
Jno Robertson /1
Att. the widdow Longs: Francis Robinson, Richd. Milner, Symon Parsons, Will Thurston, Edmund Bulstone, Joseph Wells /6

1

Sela Dorman, George Hophim /2
John Hase, Dan'll Rust, Isaack
  Marshall, Edmund Clariston non age
  /4
Joseph Peake, Robert Reeves, a slave
  called Dolle /3
Jno Ferry, Edwd. Rutledge, Jno
  Stephens, Richd. Langley, Richd.
  Jeffryes, Tho. Clinch, Jno Shaw,
  Jno Wilson, Tho. Lake, Tho. Baken
  /10
Jno Thomas, William Demett, Roger the
  Slave, Jno Gay, James Wills /5
Charles Green, Joshua Lumber /2
Charles Merriman, Henry King /2
Anthony Demondidier /1
James Roberson, Jno Underwood /2
Tho. Morris /1
Roger Reeves /1
Robt. Burgin /1
Nath. Hinchman /1
Jonas Boen, Will Story, Laurence
  Walden, Henry Lawler /4
Tho. Gilliburne /1
Abra. Vaughan, Josias Jason, Tho.
  Braghan, Steph. Atby /4
Hugh Jones /1
Thomas Minchin /1
Jno. Wilmott, Robt. Stiles, Darby
  Dyer /3
Will Ganie, James Gaslen /2
Jno. Ensor, Robt. Green /2
Edw'd Norris, Joseph Newham, Jno.
  Gusse, James Hedentan /4
Jno. Copas /1
Thomas Stone /1
John Cole /1
John Broad, Walter Halcloke /2
John Oulton, Tho. Smallwood, Dan'll
  Palmer, Nich. Hale, Geo. Chancy,
  Edw'd. Russell, Robt. Hood, and 3
  slaves, Jno. Mallony, Tom Sive and
  Grace /10
Dan'll Welch /1
Rob't Stockswill /1
Jno. Carriton, Jacob Johnson, Joshua
  Howard /3
Robert Parker, William Daves, Stephen
  Wiles /3
Anthony Johnson /1
Stephen Bently /1
Tobias Stornbarrow, John Wright /2

Rowland Thornbridge /1
Joseph Gotwicke /1
Nicholas Corbin, Edward Bone, William
  Talbott, Jno. Elmes /4

John Bevan, Constable of the
  Southside of Gunpowder Hundred
Luke Raven, Robert Linch, Geo.
  Grover, James Smithers /4
Henrich Cornelius, Edward Jones /2
Thomas James /1
Daniel Scott /1
Henrick Inloes, John Inloes, Robert
  Hakly /3
Lewis Noell /1
Robert Benger, John Murfye, Thomas
  Banks, John Burton /4
Sam'll Maxfield /1
Will: Eales, Jno. Darlin /2
Cap't. Thomas Richardson, Symon
  Bekitt, Charles Smith, Richard
  Fowler, Dan'll Jones /5
Rob't Gates /1
Laurence Richardson, Edward
  Cottenton, Nich: Congdon, John
  Duncan /4
Robert Gasquome, Jno. Taylor /2
William Wright, Thomas Vinbell,
  Benjamin Bennett /3
John Anderson /1
Edward Felks /1

A list of the tythables of the North
side of Gunpowder River hundred - 25
July 1692. Edmund Hansley
(Hausley?), Constable of the North
side of Gunpowder hundred.
At Tho. Staly: James Durham, Gilbert
  Perren, Dan'll Gasquoine /4
Thomas Jones, Charles Jones /2
William York /1
Tho. Heath, William Brooks /2
William Ebden /1
Jno. Walford, Jno. Squires /2
Will Standefer /1
James Frizell /1
John Mark /1
John Debrewlah /1
William Hill, John Hill, James
  Cowdrey /3
John Durham, John Durham Jun. /2

Richard Adams, Dan'll Danney, George
  Hancock, Joshua Wood, Joseph Loe,
  Rich'd. Adams, Jun. /6
William Lenox /1
At James Maxwell, Jeremy Hacks,
  Robert Walter, George Harthorn,
  William Westrell /5
William Dison /1
Jno. Wright /1
Robt. Olesse, Sam'll Standefer, Robt.
  James /3
Israell Skelton, Edw'd. Waters, Jno.
  Gray /3
Cornelius Harrington /1
John Rawlins, Tho. Newsam /2
Tho. Preston, James Masard, James
  Dennis /3
Sam'll Sicklemore, Will Gudgeon,
  Edw'd Elliott /3
James Thomson, Rich'd. Isaack, Jno.
  Taylor /3
Moses Groome, Jno. Harrington /2
Micha. Judd, Mathias Jewell /2
Jno. Fuller /1
Thomas Smith /1
John Love, Robert Love, Robert
  Gudgeon /3
Edmund Hansley (Hausley?), Jno.
  Tylliard, Tho. Custavin /3
At Jno. Hall: Rich'd Bright, Thomas
  Shard, Robert West, 1 slave /5
Tho. Norris /1

A list of the Taxables in Spesutia
hundred of Baltimore County - 1692.
Taken by Tho. Corde high constable
for the said year: Imprimis
Col. Geo. Wells, his son Benjamin,
  Ralph Gillion, 5 slaves /8
Tho. Browne /1
Jno. Thomson, Isaack Johnson /2
Jacob Loton, Jno. Miles /2
Will Boring /1
Tho. Williams /1
Tho. Gilbert /1
Richard Symson /1
Gideon Gambrell /1
Jno. Walstone, Geo. Morgan, Rich'd.
  Lewis, Jno. Haselwood, Tymothy
  Harse, 5 slaves /10
Will Lastin at Delse, 3 slaves /4

Rich'd Askew, Rich'd. Hambleton,
  James Mago, Martin Depost, Tho.
  Bright /5
Will Pritchard /1
Sam'll Jackson /1
Will Hollis, Joseph Jackson /2
Jno. Parker, Jno. Parker /2
Geo Smith, Joseph Lee, John Howard /3
Mark Richardson, Will Long, Welch
  Will, 1 slave /4
Will Osborne, Jno. Hall, Edw'd Wild,
  Jno. Howard /4
Antho. Drew, Garratt Toppin, Walter
  Johnson, John the Taylor /4
At Mr. Gibsons: Lewis Burman, Jno.
  Bedford, Geo. Mirritt, 6 slaves
  /10
Roger Mathews /1
Mathias Prosser /1
Adam Birchill /1
Rich'd Greene /1
Jno. Miles /1
Humphry Jones /1
Cha. Ramsey /1
Tho. Thurston, 2 slaves /3
Mr. Edw'd Boothby, Jno. Morgan, 2
  slaves /4
Tho. Greenfeild /1
Laur. Taylor /1
Rich'd Perkins /1
Robt. Drisdell /1
Tho. Prebble /1
Francis Smith /1
Lodowick Martin, Andra Highca, James
  Ives, Tho. Morris, Novell Deforge
  /5
James Philips, Geo. Gunnell, Tho.
  Lee, Antho. Demasters, Rich'd.
  Lovett, 3 slaves /8
Henry Haslewood, Will Haslewood /2
Peter Fucatt, John Cambest, Jeremiah
  Smith /3
Geo. Utye, Will Ashbye, Edw'd.
  Harply, Christopher Lathorn /4
Simeon Jackson, Jno. Jackson /2
Att Widdow Goldsmiths: Will Kettnatt,
  Will Dickers /2
Emanuell Sely /1
John Kimble, Francis Whitehead,
  Nathaniell Anderson, Richard
  Oliver /4

Sam'll Browne, Morris Neale, 1 slave
  /3
Widd: Peverell, Tho. Hagges, Barth.
  Hedge /2
Sam'll Baker, Evan Miles /2

Mr. Tho. Hedge, Henry Hedge, Jno.
  Rosby /3
Tho. Kerksey /1
Tho. Corde, Miles Hennes /2

BALTIMORE COUNTY TAX LIST - 1694
Baltimore County Court Proceedings, Liber G#1, folios 272-275

A List of Taxables in Spes Utia
Hundred in Baltimore County 1694
Mr. James Phillips, Anthony Phillips,
  Thomas Lowe, Edw. Weldy, 5 slaves
  /9
Samuel Browne, Tho. Hedges, James
  Mayo, Anth. Demaster, The boy
  Tho., 2 slaves /7
Geo. Smith, Morris Neale, 1 slave /3
Mr. Edward Boothby, Solomon Rice,
  Peter Fucatt, The boy George, 2
  slaves /6
Mr. John Hall, Emanuel Cely, Garret
  Garretson, Rob't. James, James
  Ives /5
At Mr. Willm. Osbournes: Evin Mills,
  Jno. Hall, Jno. Howard, Tho.
  Fenuck, Timothy Hurst, 1 slave /6
Mrs. Eliz. Lotton, Rich. Oliver, Jno.
  Miles, 1 slave /6
John Johnson, Isaac Johnson /2
Thomas Williams, George Morgan /2
George Gunnell /1
Tho. Bevins /1
Col. George Wells, Ralph Gillham,
  John English, The boy Phillip, 5
  slaves /9
At Mr. Gibsons: Lewis German, Miles
  Henis, George Morrit, 5 slaves /8
Mr. Samuel Fendall, Tho. Newson, 3
  slaves /5
Joseph Lowe /1
Roger Mathews /1
Mathias Prosser /1
Thomas Bright /1
Samuel Baker /1
Thomas Corde, John Haslewood /2
Richard Perkins /1
Francis Whitehead /1
John Mills /1
Humphrey Jones /1
Gideon Gamball /1

John Parker Sen., Jno. Parker Jun.,
  William Parker /3
George Hartshorn /1
Robert Walter /1
Mr. Marke Richardson, Willm.
  Reynolds, 1 slave /3
Anthony Dreco, Charles Hall 2
Mr. Willm. Hollis, Edw. Harple /2
Rich Greene, Willm. Loney /2
Rich. Askew /1
William Prichard /1
Mr. George Utie /1
Lodowick Martin /1
Simeon Jackson, Joseph Jackson, John
  Jackson /3
Francis Smith /1
Robert Drisdale, his son Tho. Jackson
  /2
Nath Anderson, Tho. Pribble /2
Henry Haslewood, Willm. Haslewood /2
Lawrence Taylor /1
Thomas Greenfield /1
Thomas Carsey /1
Thomas Gilbart /1
Richard Simpson /1
Jno. Kemboll, The Boy Peter /2

The Taxables of the South Side of
  Gunpowder Hundred. Given under my
  hand and Seal this 7th Day of Aug.
  94. Joseph Peake, Constable.
Robert Gates /1
Thomas Litten /1
Capt. Thomas Richardson, Charles
  Smith, Thomas Humbles, Thomas
  Gudgeon /4
Lawrence Richardson, John Gudgeon /2
Lawrence Gudgeon /1
Robert Gaskin /1
James Smiths /1
Simeon Parson /1
Edward Felkes, Benjam. Bennett /2

Robert Smith /1
John Anderson /1
Edw. Jones /1
Rich. Fowler /1
George Grover /1
John Bevins /1
Giles Stephens /1
John Fuller /1
John Enlowse /1
Daniel Scott /1
Henry Enlows, Abraham Enlows, John
    Cooke /3
Thomas James, Oliver Harriott /2
Luke Raven, George Hopham, Richard
    Smithers, John Northen /4
William Gudgeon /1
Joseph Peake, Rich. Millard, 2
    slaves, Willm. Horne, Edward Hooke
    Crip--- /6

A List of Taxables from the North
Side of Gunpowder Hundred. Given 7th
day of Aug: 94 by Edmond Hansley
(Hausley?), Constable.
William Standefer, Willm. Standefer
    Jun., Samuel Standefer /3
John Rawlings, James Massard /2
Thomas Preston, Richard Knight,
    Daniel Gaskin, Robert Shaw /4
John Eles /1
John Boone /1
Charles Herrington, Richard Bright /2
Tho. Norris /1
Israel Skelton, Edw. Waters, John
    Gray /3
Mr. Thomas Hedge, --- Hudrickson
    (Hndrickson?), James Trinson,
    James Dennis /4
Samuel Sicklemore, Robert Gudgeon /2
Moses Groome, Bartholomew Hedge /2
Thomas Smith /1
John Love, John Taylor /2
Charles Hewitt /1
Robert Benger, Thomas Banks, John
    Chadwell /3
Mich. Judd /1
Thomas Heath /1
Thomas Staley, James Durham, Enick
    Spinkes /3
John Cambell, Thomas Shard /2
John Devega /1

Richard Adams, Rich. Adams Jun.,
    George Hancock, Garrett Toping,
    Joseph Looe, William Nobell /6
Robert Olesse, Willm. Denton /2
John Gallion /1
Mr. James Maxwell, Martin Taylor,
    Joshua Wood, John Burnington, 2
    slaves /6
John Hill /1
John Durham, John Durham Jun. /2
William Hill, James Cowdrie, Jeremy
    Hacks /3
Cornelius Boyst /1
John Mark /1
John Debrewler /1
William York /1
James Frizell /1
WWilliam Ebden, Richard Isaac, Thomas
    Cannon /3
Thomas Jones, Charles Jones,
    Cadwaleford Jones /3
Gilbert Perring /1
John Wright /1
At Mr. Halls, Aquilla Paca, John
    Ewings, John Newell, Robert West,
    1 slave /5
Edmond Hansley (Hausley?) /1
WWilliam Churne, Wilkes Churne /2
Robert Love /1

A List of the Taxables names taken by
    Selah Dorman, Constable of
    Potapsco hundred on the South Side
    of Back River in July 1694.
(North Side of Potapsco hundred)
John Ferry, Thomas Clynch, William
    Demitt, Richard Jeffery, John
    Gibines, John Shaw, Arthur /7
Rowland Thornborow, Edward Rutlidge,
    Charles Thornborow /3
Robert Willimott, John Cooper /2
Josiah Bridge /1
David Thurston, John Elmes /2
Nicholas Corbin Sen., Nicholas Corbin
    Jun. 2
Joseph Gostwick, Humphrey Day /2
Nicholas Fitzsymons, Hangos Mekin,
    William Story /3
John Rowse, Stephen Wells, John
    Lovell /3
Tobias Starnbarrow, Theophilus King
    /2

Joseph Pelego, Nathaniel Appleby /2
Samuel Greenewood, William Tims /2
Joseph Strawbridge, John Wells /2
Thomas Durbin /1
Moses Edwards /1
Thomas Roberts, Michael Young, Willm.
　Freeman /3
John Harriman /1
Edmond Baxter, John Leakins /2
Lawrence Yosten, Thomas Lack /2
James Robertson /1
William Wilkinson, Thomas Bell,
　Richard Said, Thomas Smalwood,
　Edw. Stevenson, Edw. Cottington /6
Thomas Minching, Josias Jackson /2
Richard Sampson, Sen., Isaac Sampson,
　Rich. Sampson, jun., John Rishton,
　Rich. Longlom /5
Samuel Maxwell /1
Nicholas Poore, John, a hireling /2
James Todd, Richard Thomson, Thomas
　Bedeson /3
Jonas Bowing, sen., Jonas Bowing,
　Jun., Henry Lorah /3
Amos Evans /1
Thomas Gillibourn, Lawrence Walden /2
Nathaniel Hinchman /1
Edward Norris, John Thomas /2
Roger Reves /1
Daniel Elar /1
Thomas Morris /1
Abraham Vaughan /1
Robert Burgin /1
William Fenton /1
Tho. Richardson, Willm. Talbutt,
　Robert Reve, Jonas Williams /4
Charles Merriman /1
John Gage, William Taylor, Negro
　George, Negro Gellbede /4
John Gay, John Gaff /2
John Thomas, Doctor Roberts, Nath.
　Rixton, Negro Roger /4
John Underwood /1
Christopher Bembridge /1
John Broad, James Herrington /2
John Coale /1
Robert Hood /1
Thomas Stone, Samuel Gain /2
John Ensor /1
Robert Greene /1
Hugh Jones, James Gosnell /2

John Willimott, Derby the servt, A
　Woman Slave /3
George Cottam, James Oneal /2
John Copas /1
John Oleton, Tom the negro, Jane the
　negro, Grace the negro /4
Nicholas Hayle, Thomas Blackburn,
　Henry Butworth, Robert Stockstall
　/4
Daniell Welch, James Wells, Henry
　King /3
John Carrington, Joshua Hoard /2
Edward Scott /1
Robert Parker, William Davis /2
Anthony Johnson /1
Mich. Rutlidge /1
Andrew Anderson /1
Francis Watkins, Edward Cantwell,
　Edmond Moore /3
Christopher Shaw /1
Edward Boan /1
Michael Gormucken /1
Lewis Knowls /1
John Robertson /1
Francis Robinson, Edward Jordin /2
John Hayes, Daniel Rust, Ambrose
　Hogg, Jacob Johnson /4
Isaac Marshall /1
Daniel Swindell /1
John Roberts /1
Robert Gardner, Mich. Comworth, Tho.
　Hancock /3
Willm. Horner, Robuck Lynch /2
At Mrs. Jane Long's: John Wilkinson,
　Lancelott Poole, Joseph Wells,
　Mathew Bellamy, A woman Slave /5
Selah Dorman /1

A list of the tithables at the South
Side of Potapsco hundred
Mr. Geo. Ashman, Hector Meclane,
　Christopher Cardue, John
　Jefferyes, Henry Sheppe, 3
　slaves /8
Jno. Beecher, Joseph Cumpton, 1 slave
　/3
Rich Cromwell, Wm. Barker, Jno.
　Eaglestone, Jno. Robinson, Edw.
　Russell, 2 slaves /7
Wm. Budd, Rich Stacey /2
Mr. Tho. Hammon, Robert Hopkins, Jno.
　Thomas, 3 slaves /6

Tho. Hooker, Jacob Hooker, Darby Bran
/3
James Muray, John Scott, 2 slaves /4
John Stevens /1
Henry Wyatt /1
George Norman, Nathan'l Stinchcome /2
James Jackson /1
Steph. Hart, Willm. Hall /2
Willm. Slade, Hen. Fuz /2
Hen. Hall /1
Phillip Roper /1
Isaac Jackson /1
Christopher Cocks /1
John Bayes, Ralph Barrow, 3 slaves /5

Willm. Coventry /1
Joseph Tolson, Patrack Musse /2
Rich. Robinson, Charles Baker /2
John Lockwood, Robert Alline, Tho.
Corus, Joshua, Thomas /5
John Smith /1
James Smith, Willm. Hawkins, Stephn.
White, Samuell Smith /4
Thomas Homewood, Jno. Davis, 1 slave
/3
Thomas Knightsmith /1
Rich. Jones /1
William Hicks /1
Randall Jones /1

Baltimore County Court Proceedings, Liber G, No. 1, folio 521-527.
November Court 1695.

A True List of Taxables in Spesutia
Hundred by Lodowick Martin,
Constable.
Mr. Edward Boothby, John Jones, Wm.
Cannon, George Lester, Peter
Lester, 2 slaves /7
Solomon Rice, Peter Fucatt /2
Mr. John Hall, Garratt Garratson,
Thomas Capell, Jno. Bodkin, Darby
Bryan, Robt. Barrow, Isaac
Hadgrace, 1 slave /8
Coll. George Wells, Benjamin Wells,
Ralph Gilliam, John English,
Philemon Runagam, 5 slaves /10
Lawrence Taylor /1
Thomas Courd /1
Thomas Prebell, Nath. Anderson /2
John Combest /1
Simeon Jackson, John Jackson, Joseph
Jackson /3
Thomas Newsom, Anthony Demasters,
Georg Merritt /3
Joseph Hull Carpenter /1
Thomas Fenwick /1
John Shield /1
Thomas Greenfield /1
Emanual Ceely /1
Richard Bright /1
James Phillips, Anthony Phillips,
Edward Wildey, Willm. Fryley, 5
slaves /9
Mr. Mark Richardson, Charles Hall,
Willm. Renolds, 1 slave /4

Anthony Drew, Willm. Worgin, Edward
Moore /3
George Gunnell /1
Henry Hedge, Wm. Loney /2
Mathias Prosser /1
Roger Mathews /1
Wilkes Churn /1
At Mr. Gibsons: Daniel Palmer, Wm.
Haslewood, John Haslewood, Robt.
Gibson, Miles Hannest, 5 slaves
/10
George Hartshorn /1
William Hollis, Thomas Low /2
John Parker, John Parker jun., Willm.
Parker, Edward Harpley /4
Samuel Baker /1
Samuel Brown, Thomas Temple, 2 slaves
/4
Evan Miles /1
Willm. Pritchard /1
William Osborne, Jno. Hall, John
Howard, 1 slave /4
George Smith, Sen., George Smith,
jun., 1 slave /3
Samuel Jackson /1
Lewis German /1
William Dickson /1
Willm. Loften /1
Thomas Bevin /1
John Miles, Sen. /1
John Miles, Jun. /1
Humphrey Jones /1
John Johnson /1

Richard Perkins /1
Gideon Gamball /1
Thomas Williams /1
William Yorke, Richard Oliver, 1
slave /3
John Ramsey at Mr. Gould /1
Thomas Gilburt, Sen., Thomas Gilburt,
jun. /2
Richard Simpson /1
Thomas Brown, Henry Garner /2
Charles Ramsey /1
Thomas Bright /1
Return Cannon /1
Timothy Hurst /1
Francis Whitehead, George Morgan /2
Thomas Kennington /1
Henry Haslewood, James Ives, Thomas
Buttons /3
Robert Drisdale, Thomas Jackson /2
Mr. George Utie, Peter Borne, Bryan
Murphey, Christopher Lathain /4
John Kimball, Peter Kenton /2
Nath. Sappington /1
Francis Smith /1
Lodowick Martin, Thomas Morris /2

A List of Taxables of the North Side
of Gunpowder River. Given 5 Aug 1695
by James Frizell, Constable.
Edmond Hensley, Richard Tylliard /2
William Ebden /1
Joshua Wood /1
William Churn /1
Thomas Jones, Charles Jones,
Cadwalleford Jones /3
William Howard /1
John Webster /1
Robert Love, Willm. Gudgeon, John
Gray /3
Moses Groome, Gilbert Perrin,
Bartholomew Hedge /3
Thomas Staley, James Durham, Ralph
Eves, Enock Spinks /4
John Love, John Taylor, Nathaniel
Bevis /3
Michael Judd, Thomas Cannon /2
Thomas Heath /1
Robert Benger, John Chadwell, Thomas
Bankes /3
Charles Hewitt /1
John Cambell /1
John Rawlings, James Massard /2

Thomas Smith /1
Cornelius Herrington, William --- /2
Thomas Norris /1
William Lenox, Cornelius Boyse /2
Samuel Syclemore, John Gudgeon /2
Robert Gudgeon /1
John Ewings, Robert West /2
Israel Skelton /1
Thomas Preston, Daniel Gaskin, Robert
Shaw /3
John Eeles /1
John Mark, John Yorke /2
Aquilla Paca /1
William Hill, George Hancock, James
Cowdrey, Richard Knight /4
John Boone /1
John Durham, Samuel Durham, Daniel
Darney /3
John Hill, Edward Jesup /2
Mr. Richard Adams, sen., Charles
Adams, William Noble, Joseph Low,
Robert Walker /5
Richard Adams, jun. /1
Mr. James Maxwell, Edward Reves,
Jeremy Hacks, 2 slaves /5
Robert Olesse, Thomas Shard, William
Denton /3
John Gallon /1
John Wright /1
John DeBrewley, Oliver Yorke /2
Abrham Taylor, Mark Swift, Robert
Taylor /3
William Standefer, sen., Samuel
Standefer, Willm. Standefer, jun.,
Jno. Standefer /4
Thomas Hedge, Richard Isaac, Thomas
Gudgeon, John Thomson, Thomas
Shepheard /5

A List of Tithables for the South
Side of Gunpowder Hundred. Taken
by Edw. Jones.
Coll. Thomas Richardson, John
Richardson, James Dennis, Charles
Smith /4
Lawrence Richardson, Robert Gasquin,
James Smithers, Hosea the Freeman
/4
Thomas Litten /1
Edward Felkes, Benjamin Bennett, John
Hutts /3
Edward Jones /1

8

Robert Smith /1
John Anderson /1
Richard Fowler /1
George Grover /1
William Horn /1
Francis Dollarhide, William Mark /2
John Bevon /1
Henrick Inloes /1
Abraham Inloes /1
Daniel Scott /1
Luke Raven, John Cook, John Notham,
 Richard Smithers /4
Joseph Peake, 1 Negro /2
John Inloes /1
John Fuller /1
Thomas James, Oliver Harriott, Giles
 Stevens /3
William Wright /1

A List of Taxables on the North Side
 of Potapsco Hundred as taken in
 1695 by James Todd, Constable.
Anthony Johnson /1
Robert Parker /1
John Carrington /1
Nicholas Hayle, Thomas Bradborne /2
Daniel Welch, Robert Stogdale,
 Richard Milner, Henry King,
 Lawrence Walding, Richard Ammon /6
John Oldton, Thomas Smalwood, Edward
 Stevenson, George Chancey, John
 Roberts, Daniel Rust, 3 slaves /9
John Cole, James Harrington /2
John Broad, Joshua Howard, Darby Dyer
 /3
Thomas Stone, Samuel Gains, James
 Gosnall /3
John Copas /1
John Willmott, 1 slave /2
Hugh Jones, James Wells /2
John Ensor, John Thomas /2
Robert Greene /1
Coll. John Thomas, Nathaniel Rixtone,
 Joseph Stringall, 1 slave /4
John Gage, William Taylor, 2 slaves
 /4
Charles Merryman, sen., Charles
 Merryman, jun. /2
Roger Reves /1
Anthony Demondidieur, Henry Lowler /2
Daniel Ellard /1
Robert Burgin, John Burgin /2

John Mountfield /1
Nathaniel Hinchman /1
Thomas Gillibourn /1
Jonah Boyne, Sen., Jonah Boyne, jun.
 /2
Thomas Robarts, Josiah Jackson,
 Willm. Demett /3
Robert Willmott, Richard Slade /2
Nicholas Corbin /1
Joseph Gosicks /1
David Thurston /1
Tobiah Stamburgh, Theophilus King /2
Joseph Perrygoy /1
John Bayes, Willm. Peart, Thomas
 Smith /3
Thomas Minchin /1
William Wilkinson, Thomas Bell,
 Willm. Fraime /3
Samuel Greenwood, Anguish Mackaine /2
Thomas Durbin /1
Nicholas Fitzsymons, Richard Jeffery,
 Joseph Wells, John Goffe, Willm.
 Story /5
James Todd, Stephen Wells, Thomas
 Biddeson, 1 slave /4
John Rouse, John Welsh, John Jeffs /3
Richard Thomson /1
Lawrence Youstone /1
James Read, Nicholas Poore, Jonathan
 Marcey, John Underwood /4
Rich'd Sampson, sen., Isaac Sampson,
 Richard Sampson, jun. /3
John Leakin, John Harrymond /2
Joseph Strawbridge, Mich'll Young,
 Roebuck Lynch, Edward Cottington
 /4
Humphrey Day /1
John Ferry, Thomas May, Thomas
 Clinch, Edward Rutlidge, John
 Gibbens, Edw. Jourdan, John Shaw,
 Arthur Thomas, Christopher
 Bembridge, Thomas Lock /10
Rowl'd Tharnburgh, Charles Tharnburgh
 /2
Samuel Maxwell /1
Josiah Bridges, John Restone /2
John Gay, John Hilling /2
Francis Watkins, Edward Cartwell,
 James Hysom /3
Andrew Anderson /1
William Farfar /1

9

Robert Garmer, Thomas Hancock, Mich.
Coneyworth /3
Daniel Swinsdall /1
Selah Dorman /1
Mich'll Gormachan, John Elmes /2
Francis Robinson, George Hoppam /2
John Hayes, Ambrose Hogg, 1 slave /3
At Mrs. Long's: John Wilkinson,
Thomas Gilbert, 1 slave /3
Isaac Marshall /1
Lewis Knowles /1
John Robinson /1
Lancelott Poole /1
Michael Rutledge /1
Christopher Shaw /1
Richard Longman /1
Edward Bone /1
John Scott /1

A List of the Tithables on the South
Side of Potapsco Hundred (1695).
Thomas Knightsmith, Constable
Joseph Toulson, David Elder /2
Richard Robinson /1
John Locett, Thomas Bilson, James
Hope /3
Robert Allin /1
Charles Baker /1
Robert Rogers /1
John Smith /1
Samuel Smith, Philemon Smith /2
William Hawkins, Stephen White,
Willm. Hawkins, jun. /3
William Hicks /1
At Thomas Homewoods Plantation:
Tobias Barrington, John Davis, 1
slave /3
Thomas Dodd, Richard Madcalf, Thomas
Knightsmith, Constable /3
Richard Cromwell, William Parker,
John Eaglestone, Jonas Williams,
William Hall, Thomas Lytefoote,
Thomas Causell, The Boy Joseph, 2
slaves /10
Stephen Harte /1
Christopher Cocks, Philemon Mack
Cartey /2
Isaac Jackson /1
William Slaid /1
Henry Hall /1
Phillip Roper /1
Randall Jones /1

At Henry Constable's Plantation:
Thomas Croker, John Buckingham,
Ralph Barrow, 3 slaves /6
William Coventree /1
William Bud, Richard Stacey, William
Davis /3
Thomas Hammond, Robert Hopkins, 3
slaves /5
Thomas Hooker, Nath. Stinchcombe /2
James Murray, John Scott, John
Harris, 2 slaves /5
John Stevens /1
George Ashman, Peter Mack Clan, Henry
Shippi, Christopher Cordu, Thomas
Crumwell, 2 slaves, Willm.
Crumwell /8
Henry Wyett /1
George Norman, John Bryan /2
James Jackson /1
Elke Ridge, At John Dawsey's Quarter:
2 slaves /2

From Archives of Baltimore City

Deer Creek Hundred, John Cooke,
constable.
Col. Nat Rigbie, James Stewart,
  Emanuel Jones, Aron Johnson & 14
  slaves /18
George Bond. Col Rigbie is his
  Security /1
Skipwith Coale, Robert Miller, 6
  slaves /8
William Coale, 2 slaves /3
Chas. Worthington, 10 slaves /11
Jno Cook, his man Paul Crowny /2
Robt. Hambleton /1
Jno West /1
Jno Cooper /1
Samuel Cooper /1
Jno: Hen: Pickard /1
Jno Draper Sen'r /1
Jno Hollton /1
Fran's Collins & wife Anne /2
Edward Stapleton /1
Jno Brierly, Lawrence Cook /2
Peter Black /1
Charles Jones /1
James Cannan /1
Jno Willson /1
Edmond Gregory /1
Daniel Vail /1
Wm Goodwin & Benjamin Goodwin /2
William Richards /1
James Morgan /1
Thos Hambleton & Hen: Doyle /2
Jonathan Jones, 1 slave /2
Alex'r. MacCauley, 1 slave /2
Zac'ah Spencer & Hen: Derumple /2
Job Barns, Jno Dreyser Jun'r /2
Jos Willson, Wm MacCloud /2
Rich Wells, Senr, Rich'd Wells Jun'r,
  Guy Mare, 2 slaves /5
Gregory Farmer, Lewis Lee /2
Widow Hawkins, 2 slaves /2
Thos Rencher, Sen'r, Abram Rencher,
  Thos Rencher Junr /3
Samuel Brice Senr, James Brice,
  Samuel Brice Junr /3
Jno Rencher /1
Walter Ashmore, Joseph Rogers /2
John Smith /1
Jno Giles, 1 slave /2

Alexander Hill, Cornelius Killee /2
Samuel Lee, 4 slaves /5
Seaborn Tucker /1
Charles Bond, 1 slave /2
Wm Jenkins, Jams. Baulch /2
Jno Dunn /1
Thomas King /1
Abraham Heirs /1
Geo: Ridon, Thos Hillard /2
John Coale /1
Joseph Johnson /1
Richard Durhum, 3 slaves /4
Wm Moor /1
Matthew Shaw /1
Jno Johnson, his Son Wm /2
William Powell /1
Samuel Wallis, 5 slaves /6
Joseph Hopkins, 6 slaves /7
Joseph Jones /1
Thos Long, his man Michael /2
Thos Wells, Qu'r: slaves /4
William Hollands, Qu'r: slaves /4
Wm Vaters, Matthw Plumley /2
Jno Hawkins, Benjm. Taylor, 2 slaves
  /4
Joseph Lee /1
Samuel MacWilliams /1
Thos Young /1
Godfrey Viney /1
William Roads /1
William Wynn /1
Thos Bradley /1
Robert Craig /1
Edward Morgan, Thos Downs, 1 slave /3
Thos Johnson, Abraham Johnson /2
Geo: Williams /1
Charles Dawson /1
Roger Bishop /1
Francis Jenkins, Thos Jenkins /2
William Duley, Wm Beaver, Junr,
  Aquila Jones /3
William Beaver, Senr /1
Jno Bond /1
Thos Phalps /1
William Baker /1
William Ross /1
Thos Jones /1
Mary Warren, Widow /1
Nathaniel Giles, John Giles his
  security /1
Per Mr. John Cook,
Constable of Dear Creek Hundred

August the 1st 1737
Wm Powell, Rd Powell Sec. /1
William Beaver Sen, his son Henry sec
/1
John Greentree /1

List of Taxables of Spesutia Upper
Hundred taken by Obed. Pritchard,
Constable.
Thos Wheeler, 4 slaves /5
At Mr. Parker Halls qrs: James
  Bucher, 4 slaves /5
William Hunter, John Ringfield /2
Thos Baker /1
Thos Mitchell /1
William Robertson and Sarah his wife
/2
Samuel Smith /1
Benjamin Wheeler, Sen., Benjamin
  Wheeler, Jur, Ignacious Wheeler, 7
  slaves /10
Richard Johns, 4 slaves /5
Samuel Gover, 1 slave /2
Alexander Johnston /1
Michell Webster, 1 slave /2
Joseph Flint /1
Thos Shay, Henry Wiseman, 3 slaves /5
Roger Donahoe, Edward Hunt, 1 slave
/3
Thos. Treadaway Skuth, Thos Brasher
/2,
William Grafton, William Grafton,
  Junr, William Pike, Richard
  Meryman, 4 slaves /8
Samuel Wright /1
Alexander Thomson /1
Andrew Thomson /1
At Mr. Thos Bond Jun. Qr: Bever
  Spain, 1 slave /2
John Cauthery, Samuel Luis /2
Thomas Street /1
Samuel Fowler /1
At Mr. Rogers Mathias qr: William
  Brown, 4 slaves /5
Richd. Colsey /1
At Mr. Wilm. Bonds Q'r: Rich'd
  Marbee, 3 slaves /4
William Reese /1
Thos Pycraft, William Smith, Nathan
  Shepard, 1 slave /4
Robert Love, John Dollison, 2 slaves
/4
Charles Anderson, Sam'll Maccarty /2

Samuel Gilbert, Nicholas Dudney,
  Elias Craford /3
At Francis Ambey Sen'r, Sam'll Ambey
/1
Nicholas Bauhen, Sam'll Caws (Laws?),
  Richd. Bayley /3
James Prichard /1
Geruas Gilbert, Jun'r /1
Solomon Gallen /1
Thos Gallen /1
James Gallen, Jacob Johnson, Geo
  Purchase /3
William Perry /1
Peter Whiteaker /1
Thos Johnson, Wil'm Bonds Son, 4
  slaves /5
John Hays, William Hays /2
Henry Thomas /1
Soloman Reese, Sol Rees Jun'r /2
John Molten /1
Rich'd Mitchel /1
Thos Gilbert, Aquila Hanes /2
Mich'll Eastwood /1
William Arnald /1
James Preston, George Anderson /2
John Farmer /1
Isaac Butterworth, 3 slaves /4
John Crafford /1
William Perkins /1
Benjamin Ozbourn, William Ozbourn /2
Samuel Roos, William Bayley /2
Benjamin Deaver /1
John Johnson /1
William Hughes, John Hughes /2
Mich. Gilbert, Francis Ryley, James
  Ahers, Wiliam Tadd, 1 slave /5
Samuel Webster, Samuel Johnson, 2
  slaves /4
Richard Perkins, Isaac Perkins, Adam
  Perkins /3
John Webster William Hunbers son /1
John Benson /1
John Prelle, Samuel Gallen /2
At John Halls Mager qr: John Hawkins,
  7 slaves /8
Richard Butts /1
John Coen, Thomas Coen /2
John Durbin, John Durbin Junior,
  Mores Williams, 3 slaves /6
Henry Monday, Henry Gallion /2
William Hamly (?) /1

Auther Monday /1
John Higgison, James Star, Moses
    Star, 1 slave /4
Thomas Knight /1
John Paca Quarters: John Goddin, 3
    slaves /4
John Webster, 6 slaves /7
Isack Webster, William Graves (?),
    John Chisher, 2 slaves /5
William Crabtree, James Crabtree, 3
    slaves /5
John Walloks, Isack Jones /2
Thomas Bresher /1
Robert Clark, 6 slaves /7
John Williams /1
Edward Flanagan /1
At Mr. Elizabeth Smiths: Wintton
    Smith, 8 slaves /9
Daniel Judy /1
John Hughes /1
At Sarah Ruff, 1 slave /1
Richard Ruff, John Brown, William
    Dolin, 2 slaves /5
Daniel Ruff /1
Sam'll Silvestas Westcombers /1
Garus Gilbert, Thomas Roberson, 1
    slave /3
Isack Wood /1
Charles Wetacor (?), 1 slaves /2
At Mrs. Martha Paca Qu'r.: 3 slaves
    /3
Thomas Harass, Benjamin Yeger /2
Robert Collins, 1 slave /2
Thomas Comless (?) /1
Robert West Junior, Jothin West, Litt
    Knight /3
Robert West, Eneck(?) West /2
Robert Hawkins, Robert Hawkins
    Junior, 1 slave /3
James Craford, 1 slave /2
Edward Cooley /1
Thomas Hawkins /1
At Car'll Halls Quarters: Elick(?)
    Spenser, 3 slaves /4
Gregory Farmer, Thomas Farmer,
    Ferrill(?) Farmer /3
James Barnes /1
Daniel Preston /1
Henry Gorit(?), Daniel Cob(?),
    William Beattee, 1 slave /4
Edward Cosines (Cofines?) /1
James Cunnel /1

At Margaret Prichards: 1 slave /1
John Whitehead /1
John Hamton /1
At Mr. Aq'a Paca Qts: 4 slaves /4
Thomas Gash /1
Thomas Burkfield /1
Charg(?), Peter Farmer, Gregory
    Farmer Senr /(none shown)
Thomas Litten /1
Olds(?) Pritchard, Edward Johnson,
    Nicholas Bowles /3
Thos Mitchel Jun'r, Thos Mitchel
    Senr, sec. /1
Fred Lynn, Jno Hampton, sec. /1
Daniel Marder, Nich Bannum, sec. /1
Edmun Hays Jun'r /1

A List of Taxables by Thomas Browne,
Constable of Spesutia Lower Hundred.
Thomas Browne, John Lee, 3 slaves /5
Garrett Garrettson, George
    Garrettson, John Garrettson, James
    Garrettson, Freeborn Garrettson,
    Garrett Garrettson, 3 slaves /9
Aug't Browne, Richard Pirkens,
    Patrick Illinory, 1 slave /4
to Elizabeth Smith, William Allen, 5
    slaves /6
Edward Hall, John Hall, George
    Henrymarch, Owen Maccan, James
    Heroie, 3 slaves /10
John Thomas /1
to John Stokes, Isaac Bowers, 3
    slaves /3
Robert Courtney, John Courtney, Jonas
    Courtney /3
John Jackson, Sen, John Jackson,
    Jun'r, John Fillpott, Robert
    Wenerey /4
John Campell, Archbald Johnston /2
Samuell Pritchett, 1 slave /1
Charles Bailey /1
Martha Combess, Jacob Combess /2
Ketturah Combess, John Combess /2
to Josiah Middlemore, Sherewood Lee,
    7 slaves /8
to Sarah Cook, Jeremiah Cook /1
William Daughantie /1
to Mary Marshell, John Burton, John
    Timons, 8 slaves /10
William Grienfield /1
Henry More, Henry Arms /2

Abraham Taylor /1
James Taylor /1
Joshua Wood, John Riley, Anthony
    Jerman, 1 slave /4
Bennett Garrett, Jonathas Bayton,
    James Cosley /3
Henry Millen, Timothy Murphey, slave
    /3
William Sinkler, James Sinkler, 2
    slaves /4
George Hollandsworth, James
    Hollandsworth /2
Abraham Cord /1
Absolum Browne, James Browne, Jacob
    Cord, 1 slave /4
Thomas Farlow /1
John Mathews, Christopher Redmain, 2
    slaves /4
Thomas Gibbons /1
Roger Mathews, John Taylor, 3 slaves
    /5
Edward Mariaster /1
Robert Briarly /1
Henry Roads /1
to Daniel Ruff, John Preston, 1 slave
    /3
Edward Wakman, Zedorough O'Neale, 1
    slave /3
Thomas Deavour /1
John Macomas, William Macomas /2
to Ann Lester, George Lester, 4
    slaves /5
Thomas Litte, Alexander Parrish, Gye
    Litte, 1 slave /4
William Hollis /1
John Clark, Patrick Downing, 3 slaves
    /5
George Stokes, Joseph Hogskin, 9
    slaves /11
Jacob Hanson, 1 slave /2
William Garland, Henry Garland, 1
    slave /3
Soloman Armstrong /1
William Williams /1
John Cantwell /1
Edward Cantwell /1
John Norwill /1
John Lee /1
Thomas Cord, John Jordon /2
Oliver Cromwell, 1 slave /2
Jacob Giles, Lewes Grisley, Charles
    Williams, John Wood, 2 slaves /6

to Elizabeth Allen, 1 slave /2
Rouland Kembell, Robert Kembell, 1
    slave /3
John Hall, Junour, John Preston, John
    Wattkins, 11 slaves /14
John Hall, Esqr., Parker Hall, Giles
    Daniell, Jacob Logans, 12 slaves
    and one of them past his labour
    /16
William Smith, 2 slaves /3
to Sarah Terman, Davis Rosse, 1 slave
    /2
Perigrine Frisby, Christopher Hutton,
    1 slave /3
to Aramenta Young, Nathaniell
    Sinkler, 6 slaves /7
James Phillips, Thomas Johnston, John
    Eavens, Jacariah Rouse, John
    Welsh, 7 slaves /12
Gabril Browne, 2 slaves /3
William Osband, James Osband, 3
    slaves /5
to Sarah Henson, Thomas Smith,
    William Jackson, 1 slave /3
George Chancie, 1 slave /2
William Snelson, Robert Yeats /2
John Attkeson, John Floid, 4 slaves
    /6
Christopher Shipard /1
Thomas Donawen, Samuel Qick, James
    Basto, James Daggs /4
Joseph Yeats /1
John Kemp, Perygrine Browne, 5 slaves
    /7
to William Garland, Robert Lusby exr
    of George Drew, Zacariah Lusby, 5
    slaves /6
James Fowler /1
Thomas White, James Fish, 6 slaves /8
Samuell Hughs, 2 slaves /3
Edward Burrage /1
Thomas Treadaway, Planter /1
Richard Treadaway /1
Thomas Williamson, James Rutter /2
Adam Burchfield, Thomas Burchfield /2
to Stephen Wilkeson, Benjaman Loney,
    Richard Daukens, David Sisk,
    Clement Ozman, 1 slave /5
Francis Holland, John Cole Spegle,
    Joseph Court and Arron Porter, 8
    slaves /12
to Mary Browne, William Bozley /1

jo J. Wells Stokes, Thomas Beamsley,
5 slaves /6
Samuel Griffith, Henry Bucknall, 2
slaves /4
Capt Aq'a Peca (Paca?), 10 slaves /11

A List of Taxables of the Lower
Hundred on the North Side of
Gunpowder River taken by John Bond,
Constable.
John Paca, 2 slaves /3
James Maxwell, Christopher Divers,
John Mead, 6 slaves /9
Henry Wetherall, George Lumbard, 1
slave /3
John Dawney, James Dawney /2
Zachariah Smith /1
Robert Price /1
John Copeland, William Smith /2
William Robertson /1
Lemuel Howard, Richard Mincon, 3
slaves /5
Thomas Lomax /1
Patrick Vance /1
Thomas Cole, 3 slaves
H. Wells Stokes, William Arnup, 1
slave /3
William Savory, John Standueland, 11
slaves /13
Benjamin Legoe Sen'r, Security for
Benjm. Legoe Jun'r and John Clark
/2
Thomas Leagoe /1
Nicholas Horner /1
Erick Erickson, Robert Carlile, Peter
Whiteker /3
Aquilla Massey, George Worring,
Thomas Porter, Richard Ebbons,
John Loton, Henry Whalon, 2 slaves
/8
George York Senr, George York Junr,
John Frisel /3
Daniel Dawney /1
John Jameson, William Jameson, Elisha
Isaacs, 1 slave /4
Benjamin Cadle /1
Isaack Jackson /1
Mark Swift /1
Jacob Jackson, William Johnson /2
Thomas Brereton, Thomas Brereton
Jun'r, John Brereton /3
William York /1

Thomas Dawney, Henry Dawney /2
John Thrift /1
William Hill, William Whalon /2
Easter Debruler, William Debruler /1
John Debruler /1
John White, Joshua White /2
John Armstrong, Henry Armstrong /2
Robert Scott /1
John Hatton /1
James Isham, John Sharlock, 1 slave
/3
Thomas Cross /1
William Jackson /1
John Browne /1
Sarah Robinson, Thomas Durbin,
Tarrance Brady, 1 slave /3
Matthew Beck, Elijah Beck /2
Samuel Smith, Joseph Smith /2
Lemuel Baker /1
Indimeon Baker /1
George Tylor /1
Martha Paca, 6 slaves /6
Benjamin Jones /1
Jacob Lusby, John Fulks, 3 slaves /5
Mary Hughs, 1 slave /1
John Roberts, David Nisbet, Barnaby
Tehe, John Heley, 2 slaves /6
Hudson Davidge, 4 slaves /5
Draper Lusby, 2 slaves /3
Mary Crockett, 3 slaves /3
Joseph Mead, Sen'r, Joseph Mead,
Jun'r /2
Edward Mead, James Mead son of
Edward, James Mead son of Joseph,
James Winn /4
Spry Godfry Gunry /1
Robert Cutchin /1
Michael Martin /1
Edward Brusebanks, Abraham Brusebanks
/2
William Turner /1
John Loyd, 4 slaves, William White /6
David Carlile /1
Frances Mason, John Mason /1
John Hall, Jun'r at Joppa, William
Cooke, Thomas Browne, 4 slaves /4
William Cooke Security for Willia
Morton /1
Edward Sumner Security for John
Hambleton /2
William Copeland, 2 slaves /3
Seth Cayton /1

15

Josias Middlemore, Elea Crocket,
Richard Badham, 2 slaves /5
William Smith Senr, William Smith
Junr /2
Gilbert Crocket, 3 slaves /4
Jonathan Hughs, 2 slaves /3
Mrs. Smithers at Pooles Island, 2
slaves /2
James Presberry, John Wharton /2
Elizabeth Polson /1
Dinah Merican, John Ruff, 1 slave /2
Benjamin Bond /1
John Bond, Thomas Preston, Richard
Onion /3
William Dullam, Thomas Williamson,
Mary Tugood, 2 slaves /5
Stephen Roberts, 1 slave /2
James Preston /1

List of Taxables in the Upper Hundred
North of Gunpowder taken by Edmund
Talbott, Constable.
John Taylor, Samuel Harper, John
Pendcout /3
Robert Clark, James Latemore /2
David Carlile, 1 slave /2
Joseph Eleg /1
James Lowe, Moses Collet /2
John SherdBridge, Thomas Chill,
Charles Proser /3
Henery Phillips /1
John Somner, Thomas Marshel /2
James Standford /1
John Filler /1
William Talbott, John Talbott, 1
slave /3
Edmund Talbott, James Walters /2
Thomas Amos, William Fucks /2
At Samuell Chews Quarters: Francis
Hardy, 1 slave /2
Thomas Palmer /1
John Ward /1
Henery Hicks, John Taylor, John
Mallen /3
William HedgCock Jnr, Hope Baxter /2
At Joseph Wards: Richard Ward /1
John Everett /1
Samuel Wilson /1
Henery Donawho /1
Thomas Smithon /1
William Dimmet Jnr, 1 slave /2
Thomas Crabtree, John Crabtree /2

Lewey Pertee /1
At John Norintons: John Norinton,
Frank Norinton /2
Edmund Hays, Isek Hays /2
Thomas Hays /1
Thomas Denlowe (?) /1
Joseph Foresight, James Stapler /2
Alexander MacComas, Joseph Tylsen (?)
/2
George Bunnil /1
Isek Handey /1
John Bowen, Simon Hutchins /2
Thomas Mongomery, Richard Blood /2
James Perteele, Thomas Perteele /2
William Crabtree, William P. Cemose
/2
Richard Everett /1
Thomas foy(?) /1
Francis Freaman, James Wodkins
(Watkins?) /2
Edward Sanders, Benjamin Lofe /2
Claxin Bowen /1
Hugh Lowe /1
Abraham Jarrot, Charles Gilbert /2
Michel James /1
John Karsey /1
Samuel Deason, Benjamin Deason, John
Deason /3
At Benjamin's Wheelers Quarters: John
Stringer, 4 slaves /5
William Bradford, John Rodes, 1 slave
/3
Robert Makelwain /1
At Mary Crockets Quarters: John
Parker, 7 slaves /8
John Grimes /1
James Fugit /1
John Barton /1
John Hoper /1
William Rowe /1
Edward Toley /1
Roland Wine /1
Daniel Pecock /1
John Fuller Junior, William Burton,
Luice Demose /3
Thomas Barton /1
William Shepard /1
Walter Perdue, William Perdue /2
Edward Cox, senior, Edward Cox /2
Richard Cox /1
Joseph Cox /1
Thomas Yeates, William Yeates /2

James Ellet /1
William Gad /1
John Cookin /1
John Huggins, Thomas Yokley /2
William Ramsley /1
Robert Narne, George Philips /2
Abraham Enlowes, Enick Deason /2
Charles Simmons Senior, Charles
   Simmons, George Simons, John
   Simmons /4
John Norris, John Grear, Wm Hillard,
   1 slave /4
At Margaret Mack Demars Quarter:
   Thomas Burk, 1 slave /2
Samuel Durram, Thomas Wadsworth, 1
   slave /3
Nicholas Hutchins /1
At Walters Toleys Quarter, Roger
   Cannan, 6 slaves /7
James Dimmot /1
Suttin Sickamore /1
William Dimmot Senr, Thom Middleton
   /2
Thomas Gad, Abraham Ditto, George
   Ensor /3
Danil Shoye /1
Nemiah Hicks, John Trevis, Peter Hues
   /3
Samuel Standefor, John Morris /2
Archable Roler, Edward Page, Thomas
   Cox /3
At Look Stansberys Quarters: William
   Ditto, Henry Worinton, 4 slaves /6
Jacob Wright, Abraham Wright /2
Larrance Richardson, Walter Perdue
   Junior /2
William Sinkley, John Humphereys /2
Thomas Prise, Highriak Davis, Jones
   Night /3
At. James Mores Quarters: John Darby,
   John Caphes, James More Junr, 1
   slave /4
Charles Greane, John Canaday /2
John Greane /1
Richard Sampson /1
Danil Thomas, 2 slaves /3
William Standefer, Thomas Cutchin,
   Neafey Standefore, Esral
   Standefore, 1 slave /5

Thomas Norris, Jnr /1
John Fuller Sr, Nemiah Fuller, Henry
   Fuller /3
William Munk, John Fuller Sr,
   Security /1
Darby Henley, Richard Bolinton,
   Thomas Kunson, 2 slaves /5
John Ledgit Sr, John Ledgit Ju'r /2
Abraham Whickecor, 1 slave /2
Charles Bosley /1
Thomas Ellot, William Thomas /2
William Mitchel, William Ellot /2
Samuel Talby /1
Thomas Janson fork, Jacob Janson,
   John Fernis /3
William Macobins, 3 slaves /4
At Daniel Delaneys Quarter: 6 slaves
   /6
Robert Got /1
Morris Baker, James Hunt /2
Thomas Franklin, Thomas Wicks, John
   Chamberlin, Peater Moliney /4
Joseph Lendon, Richard Holems /2
At John Edwardes Quarter: William
   Cole, Archable Tod /2
John Standefore, William a servuntman
   /2
At John Norrises Quarter, 3 slaves /3
William Deale, 1 slave /2
At Thomas Coles quarter: John
   Carpend'r, 4 slaves /5
John Grear Sr, Moses Grer, Aquilah
   Grear, Edward Coulty /4
George Ellot Nod, Benjamin Colget,
   James Bilinsby, Cathren Shag, 13
   slaves /17
John Losson, Peater Carabone /2
Modejcap Cook /1
William Davis, Willim Pecock /2
At William Cathren, Thomas Horn,
   Samuel Warrin, 2 slaves /4
Edmund Henley, Benjamin Parker /2
Edward Bussey /1
At Edward Rnollemors Quarters: Tho
   Marshel, Martin Bueen /2
Look Wiley, Henry Taylor, Peater
   Nowel, Henery Pemlenton /4
Nathanil Shipard, William Armstrong,
   William Hunt, John Sharpe, 1 slave
   /5

John Holaway, Samuel Chamlet, 1 slave /3
Sulton Standefore, Richard Basket, Henery Jnkins /3
Samuel Wodkins Sr, Samuel Wodkins Jnr /2
Thomas Hutchins, Richard Smith, Charles Jones /3
Benjamin Jones Fork, Jacob Jones /2
John Ellot /1
Unick Burk, 2 slaves /3
Benjamin Norris, 3 slaves /4
William Amos Sr, William Amos, James Amos, 4 slaves /7
Thomas Brierwhod Sr, Thomas Turner /2
James Alin, George Edginton /2
John Nelson, Antiny Dimount /2
John Perteet Sr, John Perteet, 2 slaves /3
Richa'd Rodes, Thomas Rodes /2
Thomas Miles, John Miles, Simon Trewilliam, William Mitchel, 1 slave /5
Peater Carril, John High, 2 slaves /4
James Carril, Richard Treadwell, 1 slave /3
Nicholas Day, John Day, 5 slaves /7
Thomas Gidins, Andrew Scot, Denis Briant, 8 slaves /11
Thomas Bond Sr, John Blake, 11 slaves /13
Charles Baker Fork, Christefor Billin, 1 slave /3
At Wm Bonds Quarter, John Hilton, John Barks, 2 slaves /4
William Wiggins /1
Danil McComas, 3 slaves /4
John Swinard, William White /2
William Mackcomas, 3 slaves /4
William Hedgecock Sr, Asel Hedgecock /2
John Bond son of Thomas, George Beal, 1 slave /3
At Mr. Youngs Quarter: John Jones, 4 slaves /5
John Hutchins, John Farley /2
Peater Bond, John Page, 3 slaves /5
Thomas Bond Jun'r, 4 slaves /5
William Bond Sr, Edward Haley /2
At Mary Smiths: Jacob Grose /1
Peater Pertees, John Chalk, 5 slaves /5

Jacob Bull, John Bull, John Siah, William Wodlin, 5 slaves /9
Edward Norris, 1 slave /2
Caleb Hues /1
Danil Scot Sr, James Scot, 6 slaves /8
Daniel Smithon, Robert Clark Security /1
Thomas Allom /1
At the Widdo Peaca Quarter: 3 slaves /3
Abel Curtis /1
Thomas Brierwood Jnr, 2 servents /3
Richard Robinson, William Hays, William Robertson /3
William Perteet, 1 slave /2
William James /1
At Thomas Franklins: one man Wm York /1
William Deason /1
Wm Reeves, Rd. Jones Sec. /1
Gabriel Collins, Wm Maccomas Sec. /1
John Peacock, Rd. Caswell, Sec. /1
Benjamin Roach /1
Rd. Rhoades Jun, Rd Rhoads Senr Sec. /1
Wm. Barrett /1
Joseph Norris, 1 slave /2

A List of Taxables for Middle River Hundred (Constable not shown)
William Galloway, Edward Crisp, 2 slaves /4
Thomas Turman /1
Bes'a Foster, William Slaid /2
Benja Meed, William Meed /2
Tho Wright /1
Walter Talley, William Powell, 3 slaves /5
Hea't Pickett /1
Richard Crowell, 3 slaves /4
Joshuay Starkey, Johna'n Starkey, Jos'ey Starkey, Richard Dudbridge /4
Tho Delany, Steph. Bath, William Apelby, 1 slave /4
Bond Quarter: Rob't Elstop, Solo'n Wright, 2 slaves /4
William Delany, Thomas Delany /2
Joseph Biven /1
William Ingram /1
James Lynett (?) /1
Tho Gibens /1

Delany Quarter: Mich Desking, 3
  slaves /4
Chars. Rockhole, John Rockhole,
  Char'ls Rockhole, Joseph Therman,
  2 slaves /6
Edward Thos (Thomas?) /1
Blois Wright, Richard Grume, Tho
  Peney, Tim Cork, 2 slaves /7
Sam'll Stevens /1
William Bozelly, William Hankson /2
James Bozelly, 2 slaves /3
Ralp Broudax /1
Mik Herrenton /1
James Herrenton /1
Edward Corbin, Edward Corbin, William
  Corbin /3
Mick Corbin /1
Moses Merreman /1
Tho Huker, Elex Lemman, 1 slave /3
Rich Huker, William Barney /2
Abraham Koon (?), 2 slaves /3
Bavge (?) Trace /1
John Goshweny (?), 1 slave /2
Thomas Taler, Richard Burtch, 6
  slaves /8
William Wiley /1
Mordeca Price, George Smith, 1 slave
  /3
James Tomson /1
William Bucks /1
Joseph Bozely, John Spring /2
John Bozely, 1 slave /2
Benjamin Price, Tho. Wilmot, Joseph
  Lackes(?) /3
Benjamin Anderson /1
John Wiley, Jacob Douls /2
Daniel Deskings /1
Anthoney Cahmnes /1
Henry Mance, Thomas Cunt /2
Edward Day, Samuell Haselwood, 1
  slave /3
Samuel Maccubbin, 3 slaves /4
Isac Raven, 4 slaves /5
Luke Raven, 4 slaves /5
Francis Russel, Joseph Isac /2
Thomas Wright /1
John League, Isac Gross(?) /2
Anthony Inloes /1
Giles Stevens /1
Daniel Matheney /1
William Wood /1

William Matheney /1
Charles Pines /1
Thos Morres /1
Robert Parks /1
Ann Woodall, Joseph Brooks, James
  Bradley /2
Edward Parks /1
Samuel Wood /1
William Denton, Senior, John Denton
  /2
Perthm Mildues, John Mildues, 1 slave
  /3
William Denton, Solomon Hair Grace
  (Hargrove?) /2
William Andrew, Samuel Flewellin(?)
  /2
Thos Dollearhide /1
John Biven Senior /1, John Biven /1,
  James Arnel /1
Cris't Durbin /1
Tabi'a Cothrel, 1 slave /2
William Wright Blough, Tho Inzer,
  James Dolerhide /3
Joseph Wright /1
Anthoney Asher, Samuel Carter /2
George Presbury, Timothy Carter, 2
  slaves /4
Tho Stephens /1
John Chinworth /1
John Walson (Watson?) /1
Mary Jarman, William Jarman /2
William Wright, 3 slaves /4
Thomas Baly, Isac Hinton /2
Daniel Scott, Quarter: Francis
  Watkings, 2 slaves /3
Henry Hendrickson /1
Francis Grace /1
John Maccubbin, Edward Marshel /2
William Kings, James Carl (Earl?) /2
Robert Herreman /1
James Greer, Robert Groom /2
Mary Ingram, John Ingram, William
  Trapnell /2
Henry Peregoy /1
Samuel Stansbery Senr, Samuel
  Stansbery, Robert Thorn, Peter
  Buck, Robert Kibell /5
Walter James, William Coyer, 1 slave
  /3
John Hash /1
Richard Harred /1
Henry Adames /1

John Rogers, Charles Smith, Joseph
  Hintch /3
Thomas Kings /1
John Happy /1
William Thomas /1

A List of the Taxables in Back River
Upper Hundred taken by John Colegate.
William Wheeler, Junior, Samuel
  Wheeler, John Bidley, 4 slaves /7
Aquila Carr, Richard Stevens, 2
  slaves /4
Rees Bowen, John Haigh /2
Jonathan Tipton Jun., Martin Wright
  /2
George Hitchcock, Abraham Emblin, 1
  slave /3
Thomas Bellou (Bellow?) /1
John Osbur /1
William Brown /1
William King /1
William Banks /1
William Knight /1
William Tipton /1
Isaac Corixen (?) /1
Christ Shote, Senr, Christian Shote
  /2
Samuel Underwood /1
John Chilcote /1
William Flowers /1
Edward Shote, Benjamin Bond /2
John Robertson /1
Richard Bond, 1 slave /2
William Cross /1
Peter Bond, John Bond, 1 slave /3
At Benj Bowens Quarter: Benja Bowen
  Junr, 3 slaves /4
Jabis Murray, James Bowing /2
At Coll. Smiths' Quarter, Isaac
  Right, 8 slaves /9
Henry Satyr, William Jones, 2 slaves
  /4
Joseph Bagsman, Oystian Hawkins,
  William Smith /3
Thomas Carr, Peter Fontain, Armon
  Holt, 2 slaves /3
Francis Hinckley /1
George Haile, Benjamin Long, Nathanel
  Dedman, 2 slaves /5
Edward Stevenson, 2 slaves /3
Richard Lane, John Parrott /2
John Tie /1

Joseph Cross /1
Samuel Lane /1
Thomas Tipton /1
John Rutledge /1
William Wheler (Levey free), Wason
  Wheler, William Wheler /2
Henry Steveson, Richard Wood, 1 slave
  /3
John Stansbury, William Slomuth,
  Joseph Taylor, 1 slave /4
Richard Gott, Samuel Gott, 2 slaves
  /4
John Tipton, Amos Stokes /2
John Basey, Bartholomeu Welch /2
Thos Ford, Senior, John Ford, 2
  slaves /4
Thomas Ford Junior /1
At Doct'r Partridge's Quarter - Jacob
  Lawson, 3 slaves /4
At Doct'r Buchanons Quarter - William
  Winchester, William Watson, 2
  slaves /4
At John Gardners Quarter - Leonard
  Robertson, 4 slaves /5
To Ann Plowman - John Plowman,
  Jonathan Plowman /2
William Harvey /1
Jonathan Tipton, Levey Free, 1 slave
  /1
Capt John Cockey, William Cockey, 5
  slaves /7
Samuell Owings, 3 slaves /4
Patrick Constancey /1
Richard Pinkhaus /1
Richard Jones, William Kelley /2
At Doctr Carrolls Quarter - William
  Lewis, 9 slaves /10
Christian Gist, Thomas Casebolt, John
  Clarke, 1 slave /4
James Wells Sen'r, James Wells Junior
  /2
Thomas Wells /1
At Capt Rich'd Gist Quarter - 3
  slaves /4
Thomas West /1
John Price, 2 slaves /3
At Capt Robert North's Quarter -
  Robert Newman, 6 slaves /7
At Capt Thomas Todds Quarter, 4
  slaves /4
John Colegate, 2 slaves /3
Dennis Cole, Lewis French /2

John Daughhodey /1
George Brown, Robert Friott /2
Richard Glawson, Nehemiah Glawson /2
Benjamin Hammond, 2 slaves /3
At Coll. Cockeys Quarter, 9 slaves /9
John Wood /1
Thomas Cole, Senior, Thomas Cole,
    Junior, Christ'n Cole, 2 slaves
    /5
Nicholas Haile, Thomas Cook, John
    Spencely, 2 slaves /5
William Parrish, Senior, William
    Parrish, Junior, Edward Parrish,
    William Foxley, 1 slave /5
John Wilmott, Senior, John Wilmott,
    Junior, Richard Wilmott, 4 slaves
    /7
At John Boreings Quarters, Michel
    Conelly, 1 slave /2
John Chinewith, Richard Chinewith,
    William Chinewith, Arther
    Chinewith, Jeremiah Farmer /5
Richard Cole /1
Charles Merryman, Thomas Mash, Peter
    Hines /3
William Merryman /1
Dunkin Coleman /1
William Towsen (Towseir?), Stephen
    Lange /2
Thomas Boreing, William Burton /2
Charles Yates /1
John Cross /1
Abraham Raven, Robert Hart, 4 slaves
    /6
Thomas Stansbury, Richard Cross,
    William Grace, 1 slave /4
Thomas Matthewes Senr, John Thomas, 1
    slave /3
Thomas Matthewes, Junior /1
Charles Robertson, William Welch,
    John MacDonel /3
Thomas Right, John Cemp /2
Alexander Tansey /1

A List of Taxables in the Lower
    Hundred of Back River for the year
    1737 - 159 taxables - Staly
    Durham, Constable
Thomas Stansbury, Thomas Dagg, Daniel
    Stansbury, Joseph Wells, 4 slaves
    /8
William Hoppum /1

Paul Whitchcote, Paul Whitchcote,
    ju'n /2
Richard Gardner /1
Joseph Ward, Ju'n /1
At Edward Fotterells Q'rs - Samuel
    White, 7 slaves /8
Stephen Body, John Moore, 1 slave /3
John Long, 1 slave /2
John Roberts (Cammel?) /1
John Roberts, Junior /1
William Bond, Thomas Bolt, John
    Crump, William Plowright, 1 slave
    /5
Thomas Green, John Pickerin, Rich'd
    Carter /3
Robert Sutton /1
Staley Durham, Jarry Cook /2
Daniel Ward /1
At Mary Hillens - 1 slave /1
Joseph Taylor, 5 slaves /6
Benjamin Knight, James Hayes, Francis
    Hines /3
John Royston /1
Robert Love Pitslow /1
David Robeson, Francis Armstrong /2
Watkins James /1
Richard Merchant /1
Dutton Lane, Thos Boreing, 3 slaves
    /5
Solomon Hillen, James Burk, 3 slaves
    /5
Philip Sindall, Jacob Sindall, Samuel
    Sindall /3
Thomas Biddison, Jarvis Biddison, 1
    slave /3
William Johnson, William Goddard /2
Thomas Broad /1
Robert Maxwell /1
At Robert Norths Q'r - Geo Rose, 2
    slaves /3
William Fitch /1
Christopher Duke /3
William Duke, Abr'a Durham /3
Thomas Davis /1
Thomas Harris, William Wilkes, James
    Cooper /3
Jno Gregory, Thos Anderson /2
John Harryman, Valentine Carback,
    Philip Carback, Thos Sing /4
Thomas Hines, 4 slaves /5
Peasley Ingram, 9 slaves /10
Selah Barton /1

Luke Stansbury, Tobias Stansbury,
Robert Frost, Thos Mitchel, Alex'd
Reed, Edward Dell, 4 slaves /10
Joseph Thomas, Zach'a Richards,
Christ'a Sutton, 1 slave /4
George Harryman, Francis Thornbury,
Jno Fenix, Robert Boyd /4
William Norton /1
Charles Thomas /1
Thomas Sligh, Thos Caton, Nicho.
Coleman, Jno Davis, Alex'd Young,
John Chamberlin, 1 slave /7
Walter Dallas, Benj Curtis /2
At Sarah Crooks - 1 slave /1
Samuel Ormond, Richard Winstone /2
Cornelius Angling /1
Christ'a Shaw, And'r Anderson /2
Christopher Durbin Shaw /1
Richard Hendon /1
Jno Marhorue, Jno Brogdon /2
James Brown /1
Thomas Sheredine, William Tweedie,
Henry Cross, 5 slaves /8
To Frances Mason - Joseph Clutter
Cuck /1
Thos Slight, 1 slave

A List of Taxables of the Upper
Hundred of Patapscoe - 1737.
Source: Archives of Baltimore
City, Reference 1737 - Paper # 10.
Capt Richard Gist, Joseph Dean,
Thomas Cubberly, John Morgan, 1
slave /5
Col William Hammond, Haymond Hammond,
John Edwards, Simon Friend, 3
slaves /7
William Rogers, Stephen Gill, Joshua
Hall, Lewis Lett, 1 slave, James
Pitman /6
George Buchanan, Paul Young, Robert
Pinkstone, Nathaniel Young, James
Kelley, 3 slaves /8
Charles Ridgely, John Arnall, Isaiah
Okeson, Joseph Okeson, Obadiah
Okeson, 5 slaves /10
John Moale, Robert Buston, James
Avis, William Davis, 7 slaves /11
Wm Worthington's Quarter - James
Serjeant, 3 slaves /4

Samuel Hyde's Quarter - Wm
Mattingley, Wm Bandycoat, 20
slaves /22
Benjamin Tasker, Quarter - Wm Odall,
Roger Williams, 6 slaves /8
Thomas Hands /1
John Griffin /1
William Wells /1
William Fell /1
Thomas Graham /1
John Hurd, John Ayers, 1 slave /3
Robert Chapman senr /1
Joseph Cromwell, William Bell, Thomas
Hedgell, Richard Pope, William
Thompson /5
George Ashman, 3 slaves /4
John Stinchcombe, Josiah Marsh /2
John Parrish, Daniel McDaniel, 3
slaves /4
Roger Turner, Samuel Leach /2
John Goldsmith, William Smith /2
Anthony Young /1
Thomas Woodward, John Eckles, John
French, George Herbert /4
Joseph Hooper, Evan Jones, Abraham
Hay, John Baker, George Goatley,
Thomas Logsdown, John Pell, 3
slaves /9
George Walker, Anthony Baker, David
McCarright, John Keith, 4 slaves
/8
William Pearce, Robert Constable
John Spicer, Edward Spicer /2
John Levis /1
Edward Lewis /1
Philip Jones, Quarter - 3 slaves /3
Charles Hissey /1
Jacob Hurd /1
Henry Butler, Senr, Henry Butler,
Junior /2
John Pilly /1
John Dorsey's Quarter - Benjamin
Dorsey, 2 slaves /3
John Wright, 1 slave /2
Nathan Richardson, 2 slaves /3
Richard Richardson 5 slaves /6
Thomas Richardson, 2 slaves /3
John Owings, Benjamin Johnson, 2
slaves /4
Henry Owings, William Blank /2
Thomas Floyd, 1 slave /2
John Corlcutt /1

Thomas Watts, George Cancey /2
James Bannacar and his wife /2
Anne Randall, Roger Randall, John
  Robertson, 5 slaves /7
Emmanuel Toale, 1 slave /2
Maurice Baker, Alexander Baker /2
Joseph Miller /1
William Miller /1
John Macclan & a shoemaker /2
(shown elsewhere scratched out as:
  Jno Maclane security for a
  Shomaker)
Amey Townsend, William Macclan,
  Steptoe Clark, John Hays /3
James Gardner /1
William James, John Murphy /2
Michael Hodgkiss, John Sinclow /2
Henry Hancock, William Lewis, Thomas
  Wright, Thomas Price, William Carr
  /5
John Moody /1
Daniel Ragan /1
George Bailey Senior, John Bailey,
  George Bailey Junior, Macclan
  Bailey, 6 slaves /10
Richard Taylor, Joshia Holt /2
Cooper Oram /1
Joseph Arnall /1
Jeremiah Stilwell, Senior, Jeremiah
  Stilwell, Jr. /2
James Spurr /2
Sabra Thomas /1
William Rayman /1
Arthur Dunn /1
Sarah Lett /1
Susannah Lewis, Job Lewis, John
  Lewis, Humphry Lewis /3
Richard Acton, Senior, Richard Acton
  Junior /2
William Ricks /1
John Castrope, Charles Payto, Henry
  Ruttor /3
Stephen Onion, John Sanders, Nicholas
  Gay, Joseph Gray, 1 slave /5
John Johnson /1
John Stevens /1
James McDaniels Quarter - Matthew
  Thorp, Daniel Fellows /2
John Wooden, 1 slave /2
Elizabeth Gill, Edward Gill /1
Benjamin Duncan /1

John Wilmott's Quarter, John Ridgely,
  2 slaves /3
William Wooford, Charles Kelly /2
Samuel Meredy /1
John Price, Thomas Levens /2
Abraham Eaglestone, Daniel Gall /2
Patrick Kelly /1
William Roberts /1
Peter Magers /1
Richard Fowler /1
Thomas Bond, Peter Darby /2
John Roberts /1
William Flemming, Benjamin Lonly /2
John Welch /1
James Welch /1
Edward Reston, 3 slaves /4
Edward Tilley, 4 slaves /5
John Gardners Quarter - 3 slaves /3
Mayberry Helms, William Jenkins,
  George French, Ezekiel Miller /4
Peter Johnson, 1 slave /2
Sarah Parrish, Richard Parrish,
  Richard Clark, Matthias Peeke /3
William Lettle /1
Christopher Treakle /1
Thomas Spicer /1
John Gill, James Bailey, William
  Stiles, 1 slave /4
Dr. Chas Carroll Quarter - Moses
  Maccubbins, Alexander Drummer,
  Jacob Lewis, Barty Fuller, 8
  slaves /12
John Carroll, Roger Carroll, John
  Maccoy /3
Samuel Durbin /1
Rees Thomas /1
John Hagan, Cassandra Giles Sec'y /1
Robert Riddle /1
Zach Maccubbins, John Clark /1
Thomas Lennox /1
John Heddin /1
Robert Chapman Jun'r /1
William Hughes, John Holton /2
Principio Iron Works - Jacob Young,
  Thomas Leakins, William Garratt,
  John Burns, James Brown, William
  Fanrell, William Cane, Daniel
  Deputy, Joseph Merchant, John
  Cappere, William Chambers, Edward
  Betty, Nicholas Garey, 12 slaves
  /25

Benjamin Tasker Esq & Company:
Alexander Lawson, Richard Croxall,
Edmund Vade, Thomas Cockram, James
Gill, Florance Keith, Philip
Kelly, Thomas Easton, John
William, Timothy Hamilton, Richard
Cox, Francis Bland, Humphry Lane,
Hugh Peters, John Chubb, Samuel
Stevens, Henry Carter, Thomas
Kelly, Thomas Coram, Zach
Maccubbins, Henry Smith, George
Brown, Eleazer Cogill, Murrell
Allen, Thomas Key, Robert Dutton,
Benjamin Culver, Thomas Launded,
Samuel Jarviss, George Clifton,
James Flannagan, James Baker,
James Moale, John Scott, John
Cambell, Evan Humphrys, William
Wasson, William Harrison, Richard
Bunidge, Hugh McDaniel, Henry
Barnard, John Spurgin, Anthony
Byrne, 42 slaves /85

A List of Taxables in Patapsco Lower
Hundred Taken by Lloyd Harris,
Constable - 1737
William Fell, Jonathan Ellenworth, 3
slaves /5
Redmond Dearing /1
John Boreing, John Pell, Sushanna
Sullevent, 3 slaves /5
William Carter /1
John Woolf /1
Henry Fishpaw /1
Thomas Woodwards Quarter - Thomas
Speaks, (torn)en Dorset, 1 slave
/3
Benjamin Tasker Esq & Company -
Robert Huckle, Philip Pew, 3 men
slaves /5
James Powel, Francis Spredox, Thomas
George /3
Buckler Bartridge /1
Nicholas Fitzimonds /1
Samuel Smith /1
John Baxter /1
Jonass Robbinson, William Robbinson,
John Bradley, John Drapier /4
Benjamin Bowen, Senior, Benjamin
Jones, 2 slaves /4

John Gardner, John Baylis, 7 slaves
/9
Tobias Stansbury, Bowen Stansbury,
Thomas Nevill, 1 woman slave /4
John Sayth /1
William Gaine, William Newman,
William Gaine, Junior /3
Patrick Lynch, Benjamin Pawling, 2
slaves /4
Capt Robert North, William Lord, 2
slaves /4
Edward Sweeting /1
At Thomas Slighs Quarter - John
Clawsey, Samuel Davis, Thomas
Hines /3
Widdow Harriman, John Norton, Richard
Norton /2
Zacha Gray, 2 slaves /3
Richard Demit /1
Robert Wilkieson, Thomas Fenwick,
Silvanus Barlo, 1 slave /4
William Linch, John Skinner, 1 slave
/3
Jacob Rowles, Richard Wingfield, John
Funnel /3
Phillip Jones, Richard Hardeman,
William Kibble, John Dean, 2
slaves /6
Richard Galloways Quarter - Samuel
Fort, Thomas Gibbons, John Smith,
6 slaves /9
Luke Trotton, Thomas Bradley
(scratched out), John Fawday
(scratched out), 1 slave /2
John Rottenburry, Henry Pemberton,
Robert Cooper, 1 slave /4
Captain Todd, Francis Patty, Nicholas
Gash, Hanna Shaw, 7 slaves /11
Richard Ireland, John Hiser, Samuel
Haden, Antho Durant, Sible Durrant
/5
Thomas Jonas, Richard Robison /2
Charles Shaw /1
John Shaw, Thomas Shaw, John Bayes /3
James Wood /1
Nathaniel Darby, Luke Darby, Lazarus
Rogers /3
John Connnecan, John Rogers /2
Godfrey Gash, Conro Gash, Enost Gash
/3
John Sampson, James Bagford /2

Samuel Harriman, John Harriman /2
William Smith /1
Daniel Stansburry, William
  Stansburry, Francis Thornburry, 2
  slaves /5
Solomon Shields /1
John Watts /1
John Eaglestone, Thomas Hudson, 2
  slaves /4
Francis Rider /1
John Serjant /1
Edmond Baxter /1
Henry Oysten /1
John Bowen, Senior, 1 slave /2
Robert Burgwin, Senior /2
Benjamin Bowen, Junior, John Bartin
  /2
John Bowen, Junior, Benja Cole, 2
  slaves /4
Jonas Bowen, Edward Watts /2
Edward Peregoy, Joseph Green /2
Joseph Peregoy /1
Robert Green, John Green /1
George With /1
William Rawlings /1
Bray Plat Taylor, John Gaine /2
Samuel Maxfield, P'a Lovington,
  Jonathan Glosop /3
Nicholas Gostwick /1
Samuel Maccubbins, Samuel Elston,
  John Cooper /3
Jasper Hall /1
Charles Gorsuch, Senior, Charles
  Gorsuch Junior, William Gorsuch, 2
  slaves /5
William Green /1
John Ensor, William Ensor, Samuel
  Webb, 2 slaves /5
George Cole, Senior - Levy Free,
  George Cole, John Haycroft /2
John Merriman, Junior, William
  Holmes, Thomas Fox, 1 slave /4
Thomas Gosuch, Lovelace Gosuch, Alex
  Gater, 1 slave /4
Alex'andr. Grant, Alexandr. Keeth, 3
  slaves /5
Thomas Wheeler /1
William Hall /1
John Evans /1
Job Evans & John Cook /2
Morgan Murray /1
John Board /1

John Stevenson, 1 slave /2
Rd King Stevenson, Frederick Hopkins,
  2 slaves (torn)
William Barney, 3 slaves /4
Samuel Merriman, John and Isaac
  Smith, 3 slaves /6
Thos Fra Roberts /1
Matt Hawkins /1
the Widdow Hale - Neal Hale, 2 slaves
  /3
John Merriman, William Hilon, John
  Oliver /3
John Edwards, Jas Sanner /2
Thomas Rutter, Thomas Hooster, Samuel
  Kisley /3
Jonathan Hanson, Thomas Seymore, 1
  woman slave /3
Lloyd Harris, James Mash, Alexandr
  Hume
Mary Shaw, Luke Trotten Sec /1
John Dott, Phill Jones Sec /1
John Clagill, Wm Hall his Sec /1
Benj Knight Planter, John Board Sec
  /1
Tho. Rogers - William Carter Sec /1
Ric'd Williamson, Samuel Fort Sec /1
Nicholas James, William Fell Sec /1

The True List of Taxables Belonging
  to the Soldiers Delight Hundred -
  1737, Thos Lodgsdon, Constable in
  the behalf of Law Hammond
Cur'l William Hammond Qr - Edward
  Oisller, 4 slaves /5
Jos'us Murray, Jos'h Murray, And'r
  Braford, Wm Newell, John Berrey, 4
  slaves /9
John Jenkins, Richard Green, James
  Allen, John Walker, 4
Wm Rowles, Wm Welsh, 1 slave /3
George Ogge, Wm Willson, 3 slaves /5
Philip Jones q'r - John Shaw, 3
  slaves /4
John Oricks q'r - 3 slaves /3
John Paca q'r - Wm New, 1 slave /2
Christop'r Randall, 3 slaves /4
Wm Hamilton, John Hamilton, Toney
  Bush, John Black, 2 slaves /5
Cornelus Howard /1
Jos'a Howard, 1 slave /2
George Baley Durlyface /1
Charles Motherby, John Ward /2

John Hawkins, Robert King /2
Capt Rich'd Gist q'r - Wm Sebrooks, 2
    slaves /3
George Miller /1
Rich'd Mash /1
Nath'l Davis /1
John Baker, Dom'n Baker, Abner Baker
    /3
Wm Gosnell /1
Peter Gosnell /1
Jos'a Sewiell Jr, Jos'a Sewiell Sr,
    Christop'r Sewilel /3
Edward Parrish /1
James Griffith /1
Moris Gosnell /1
And Dorsey /1
Thos Portor
Rich'd Rutter /1
Thos Brothers /1
Zeb'a Baker, Robert Iseril /2
William Baker, Regimlick Baker,
    William Baker /3
John Peddicoate, Dorsey Peddicoate /2
Nath'l Ayres /1
Stephen Willkien (Willkson?) /1
Robert Elsom /1
Owin Williams /1
John Tye, John Bell, William Arnold
    /3
Capt John Risteau, 3 slaves /4
Thos Gist /1
John Bowin, James Hane /2
Edward Stocktell, William Banister /2
John Stockstill, Thos Stockstill /2
Capt Rich'd Owings, Stephen Owings /2
Francis Dorsey, Benj'a Borddiace /2
Gilbert Isieril /1
William Peddicoate, David Dehay,
    Philip Edward /3
Edward Thomas, Henry Pearce /2
Leakle Walker /1
Edm'n Howard, 2 slaves /2
John Buckenham, John Peninton /2
Nath'l Stinchcomb, 2 slaves /3
Danil Rowling, Sr, Danil Rowling Jr
    /2
Stikle Gladman /1
Benj'a Davis /1
Tho's Rowile /1
George Roberts /1
Thomas Parker /1

Par: Neale, Jor'a Neale /2
Charles Wells, Anthony Arnold, 1
    slave /3
Nathaniel Gist, James Turner /2
Rich: Jacks, Nich's Peddicoate /2
Cap Vrile (Vaile?) q'rs - 1 slave,
    William Murphey /2
Thomas Wells /1
Jos'a Owings /1
Jos'h Curnelus /1
John Mash /1
Joseph Bird, Joseph Smith /2

Lloyd Harris for his Inquisitions
Job Evans for 24 squerrel heads, omitted to be allowed for last year
William Parks for printing the laws
James Fowler for maintaining Jonathan Howell a county patient six months, 8 days
Elizabeth Hardyman a pensioner for his maintainouse last year
Thomas Jenings assignee of John Nichols Cryer of the Assize Court for Cryers fees
Joshua George for Criminal fees
George Elliott Pork Gim 1 for maintaining Mary Mattux a pensioner, 7 months and burying her
John Woolley for burying Thomas, a poorman
Robert Green for maintaining Sarah Fox for about 5 weeks
Edward Walreman (Waheman?) in part for attending and applying Doctors means to the County patients as per agreement
George Buchanan for ditto
John Carpenter for maintaining Prudence Cox and Orphan child 3 months
Benjamin Bond for maintaining John Chambler a pen'tr ... (torn) months
Robert Price for work done to the Court House
Ann Clegg a petr for her maintain, last year
James Moore for the maintain'e of Sarah Turbell a pentr last year
Robert North for two levys overcha(rged) last year
John Lloyd for maintaining Samuel Ulph from the last Feb til 10 May and burying him.
Edward Mead for maintaining Jno Chambla, a pentr, 6 months
Edward Cooley for maintaining and burying John Carpenter and Aron Jones, pentrs.
Joseph Bevans for maintaining Sarah Beavans, a pentr in the year 1736 and 1737.

Thomas Sligh assignee of Frances Mason for Entertaining March, June and August County Court Grand Jurors.
Attending as grand jurors: William Bradford, Thomas Brown, Richard Caswell, John Clark, John Durbin, George Elliott (Land Nod), Thomas Franklin, Peregrine Frisby, Thomas Giddens, Christopher Gist, Nathaniel Gist, Richard Gist, George Ogg, Stephen Onion, Samuel Owings, Aquilla Paca, John Paca, Charles Ridgeley, John Risteau, Daniel Scott, Thomas Sheredine, Thomas Sligh, George Stokes, Henry Wetherall
Receiving bounty for wolfs heads: Thomas Bond, assignee of Fra Freeman; Thomas Bond, assignee of Wm Willbourn; Christopher Gist; Richard Gist, assignee of John Hance Steelman; Richard Gist, assignee of John White; Richard Gist, assignee of Joseph Cornelius; Josephus Murray; Robert Owings; Benjamin Price; James Rigbie, assignee of Indian Peependo; Nath Rigbie Junr, assignee of Indian Joshua; Nath Rigbie, assignee of Geo Coale; William Rogers, assignee of William Roberts; Skelton Staniford; John Webster, assignee of Tho Brashier; Thomas Wells.
Richard Gist assignee of John Spicer for nurseing William Newell 2 weeks & burying him.
James Boreing for nurseing Mary Cox's child about 6 weeks.
Thomas Sligh assignee of Frances Mason for keeping Gunpowder Ferry last year.
Richard Caswell, a cor(o)ner for 5 inquistions.
Nicholas Day for entertaining March County Court Grand Jury in 1730 omitted.
Samuel Westcombe for entertaining Marg't Gent, a pentioner 16 months & burying her.
William Hammond for last levys.

James Elliott for 51 squirrel heads omitted last year.

William Hammond for John Thomas's Levy that he cannot get.

For attending as pettit jurors: George Ashman, John Battenbury, John Bayley, Joseph Baysman, John Bond, John Bond (Gunpowder Neck), William Bond, Benjamin Bowen, John Bowen, William Bradford, Jacob Bull, David Carlile, John Clark, John Cook, William Copeland, Joseph Cromwell, John Ensor, Gregory Farmer, William Fell, Thomas Richardson Forrest, William Galloway, George Garretson, Bennet Garrett, Thomas Giddens, Michael Gilbert, John Gill, Richard Gott, William Grafton, Thomas Green, Samuel Griffith, Nicholas Haile, Edward Hall, Parker Hall, John Hawkins, Darby Henley, Solomon Hillen, Thomas Hines, Francis Hinkley, John Hurd, Thomas Johnson, Thomas Johnson (fork of gunp'd), Benjamin Jones, William Lynch, Daniel MacComas, John Maccubbin, Samuel Maccubbin, Samuel Maccubin jun, John Matthews, James Maxwell, Bartholomew Millkeye, John Moale, Benjamin Norris, Edward Norris, Robert North, Joshua Owings, Aquila Paca, John Paca, William Petticoat, George Presbury, Abraham Raven, Isaac Raven, Thomas Richardson (Gun' Forrest), Jonas Robertson, Charles Robinson, Richard Robinson, Richard Rubfe(?), ..ry Satyr, William Savory, Daniel Scott, John Searjant, Thomas Sligh, Darby Stanley, George Stokes, Samuel Stowell, John Sumner, Edmond Talbott, William Talbott, Thomas Taylor, John Tipton, Thomas Todd, Henry Wetherall, John Willmott, Joshua Wood, Samuel Wood, John Wright

Elizabeth Smith for maintaining Mary Nicholes about 7 1/2 mos & burying her.

Job Evans for maintaining Sarah Evans, a pentioner from last March.

Ann Anderson for burying Johannah Trapnall, a pentioner.

Samuel Ogle, Esqr. for Chancellers fees.

Edmond Jennings for Secretary's fees.

Daniel Dulany for attorney General's Criminal fees.

Bounty for wolf's heads: Richard Gist assignee of John Hance Steelman, George Ogg assignee of John Hance Steelman.

Bounty for squirrill's heads: Richard Acton, Senr, William Amoss, Charles Anderson, William Andrews, Solomon Armstrong, Anthony Arnold, Joseph Arnold, Anthony Asher, Abraham Ayrs, Indemiah Baker, Samuel Baker, William Baley, Nicholas Banoom, William Barney Sen, Ford Barns, Job Barns, Thomas Barreton, John Barton, Joseph Baseman, William Bentley, Joseph Bevans, Captain William Bond, Peter Bond, Richard Bond, Jno Bond(Gunpowder), Thomas Bond (Potapsco), John Bond son of Thomas, John Bozley, William Bozley, Samuel Brice, Absolum Brown, George Brown, William Brown, John Buckingham, Adam Burchfield, Henry Butler, Edward Cantwell, George Chancey, Robert Chapman, John Chinworth, John Clark Levil, William Coale, John Cockey, Thomas Cole (Gunpowder), James Cooke, Abraham Cord, John Craford, James Crassord (Crafford?), Joseph Cromwell, John Cross, Kittura Cumbest, Thomas Cumbest, Nathaniel Darley, Thomas David (David Thomas?), William Davis, Edward Day, Richard Deaver, Junr, Richard Deaver, Senr, Thomas Deaver, Richard Demmett, William Denson, Thomas Dulany, John Durbin, Samuel Durham, Anthony Enloes, John Ensor, John Fleming, Thomas Floyd, Perrigrin Frisby, James Fugate, William Gallaway,

Bennet Garrett, Garrett Garrison, Michael Gilbert, Nathaniel Gist, Thomas Gorsuch, Richard Gott, Zacharick Gray, Thomas Greeham, Thomas Green, William Greenfield, John Griffin, Samuel Griffin, John Hall, Parker Hall, John Halton, Samuel Harryman, William Harvey, Matthew Hawkins, Thomas Hawkins, Josias Hendon, Henry Hendrickson, Francis Hinckley, Thomas Hines, William Hitchcock Junr, William Hitchcock Senr, Francis Holland, John Hoofer, Nicholas Horner, Samuel Hughes, William Hughes (Spesuity Upper Hundred), John Hutchins, Thos Hutchins, Peasley Ingram, Richard Ireland, John Jackson, William Jackson, Peter Johnson, Thomas Johnson, Thomas Jones, Patrick Kelly, Thomas Kemp, John Lawson, John Lee, Benjamin Lego, Thomas Litton, Thomas Long, James Low, Patrick Lynch, Alex'd. MacComus, William MacComus, John Macconican (Potapsco), James MacDaniel, William Manor, Frances Mason, Aqa Massey, Samuel Maxwell, Andrew McGill, Edward Mead, Dinah Merriken, Charles Merryman, Thomas Miles, Bartholomew Milhuse, Richard Mitchel, Thomas Mitchel, Samuel Moreday, Benjamin Norris, John Norris, Thomas Norris, Junr, Cooper Oram, Benjamin Osborne, Henry Owings, John Owings, Samuel Owings, Henry Oyston, Aqa Paca, John Paca, John Parrish, Edward Pawley, William Perry, James Phillips, John Polett, John Pribell, Robert Price, Obadiah Pritchet, Christopher Randal, Abraham Raven, Isaac Raven, Luke Raven, Daniel Regan, John Renshaw, Thomas Renshaw, William Richards, Thomas Richardson (Potap), Charles Ridgley, James Rigbie, George Rigdon Senr, John Risteau, Henry Roads, John Roberts (Joppa), Jonass Robinson, Charles Rockhold, William Rogers, Francis Russel, Thomas Rutter, Edward Sanders,

William Savory, Daniel Scott Senr, Thomas Shea, Thomas Sheredine, John Simkins, Philip Sindall, Thomas Sligh, Samuel Smith, Hillen Soloman, Thomas Spicer, John Stansbury, Thomas Stansbury Senr, Giles Stevens, Thomas Stevens, Henry Stevenson, Richard King Stevenson, Edward Stevinson, John Stinchcomb, George Stokes, Edward Sweeting, John Swinyard, Walter Tally, Alex'd. Tanzey, Abraham Taylor, Benjamin Taylor, James Taylor, Joseph Taylor, Charles Thomas, David Thomas (Thomas David ?), Andrew Thompson, Edward Thorp, Edward Tilly, John Tipton, Thomas Tipton, William Tipton, Thomas Todd, Samuel Tolby, William Towson, Luke Trotton, Thomas Watts, John West, Robert West Junr, John White, Charles Whitear, Peter Whitear, Robert Wilkinson, Thomas Williamson, Charles Wills, James Wood, Jos Wood, Samuel Wood, John Wooley, William Wright forrest, Joseph Yates

Nathan Rigbie his aud(it) of crim'l fees

Martha Paca for maintaining Ruth an orphan child last year.

Richard Gist, assignee of Joseph Ward for Criminal fees.

Richard Gist, assignee for Joseph Ward for his annual allowance and beating the drum.

Richard Deaver Junr for maintaining Francis Dallahide 3 months

Josephus Murray for fees paid to J. Wells Stokes for John Berry a criminal servant.

Thomas Sligh for fees paid for John Berry, a criminal servant.

Humphrey Wells Stokes for Criminal fees.

Humphrey Wells Stokes for his annual allowance.

For siting fees: Thomas Brerewood, Richard Coswell, Richard Gist, Parker Hall, Phillip Jones, Aquila Paca, Nathan Rigbie, John Risteau, Thomas Sheredine, Thomas Todd

29

John Hall for fire wood, candles and
a room in laying the levy.
William Cook for work done to the
prison.
John Hall for lost levys.

ST. THOMAS PARISH

Contributors to the building of The
Garrison Church of St. Thomas Parish,
Garrison Forest, in 1743 (From
Sketches of the History of St. Thomas
Parish by Rev. Ethan Allen, D.D.,
Baltimore, New York: James Pott & Co.
1898.

George Ashman, John Bailey, John
Baker, John Bell, Benjamin Bond,
Peter Bond, Richard Bond, Thomas
Bond, Benedict Bourdillon, John
Bowen, Anthony Brayford, William
Brown, Robert Chapman, Sr., Edward
Choate, Thomas Coale, Jr., William
Cockey, Joseph Cornelius, Joseph
Cromwell, John Derample, Penelope
Deye, Francis Dorsey, Edward
Fotterall, George Bailey Gar, Stephen
Gill, Nathaniel Gist, Thomas Gist,
Peter Gosnell, Capt. Samuel Gray,
Neale Haile, Nicholas Haile, John
Hamilton, William Hammond, Thomas
Harrison, John Hawkins, Mayberry
Helm, Edmund Howard, William Lewis,
Darby Lux, Peter Maigers, William
Murphy, Joseph Murray, Jr., William
Newell, George Ogg, Joshua Owings,
Samuel Owings, Stephen Hunt Owings,
Dorsey Peddicoart, William
Petticoart, Jona. Plowman,
Christopher Randall, Charles Ridgely,
John Risteau, Henny Seabor,
Christopher Sewall, Joshua Sewall,
John Shippard, John Simkins, John
Stinchcomb, Nathaniel Stinchcomb,
John Thomas, John Thrasher, Jona.
Tipton, William Tipton, Richard
Treadway, Hector Truley, Thomas
Wells, Stephen Wilkinson, Richard
Wilmott, John Wood

Wardens and Vestrymen, St. Thomas'
Parish. V - Vestryman; W - Warden; R
- Registrar; D - Delegate to the
Diocesan Convention.

George Ashman, V 1745, 1746, 1750
William Beazeman, W 1746
Benjamin Bond, V 1749-51
John Bond, V 1745-47
Peter Bond, V 1748-50
Richard Bond, W 1747
Nathan Bowen, V 1745-47
Arthur Chinneworth, W 1749
William Cockey, V 1745
John Ford, V 1749-51
John Gill, V 1745, W 1746, V
1754-56
Stephen Gill, W 1750
Robert Gilresh, V 1748-50
Thomas Gist, V 1747-49
William Gist, W 1748
Peter Gosnell, W 1745
John Hamilton, V 1745-46
William Hamilton, V 1746
John Hawkins, V 1746, 48, R
1748-49
Cornelius Howard, W 1745
John Hurd, W 1748
William Kelly, W 1749
Henry Morgan, V 1747
Thomas Norris, V 1746-48
George Ogg, W 1750
Capt. Nicholas Orrick, V 1750-52
Joshua Owings, V 1745-46, W 1747
Samuel Owings, V 1750-52
Christopher Randall, R 1745-47
Nath'l Stinchcomb, V 1745-46
John Wilmott, Jr., V 1747-49
William Worthington, V 1749

PETITION

After 1750 (May 25?) Various Inhabitants of Baltimore City and County. To
Governor Samuel Ogle and the Assembly.
For want of exactness in laying out, Baltimore will not, upon being
resurveyed, conform to its original stakes; some of the improvements on most
of the lots, surveyed from the outline of the town, will be found in the
streets and on other lots; the church will stand partly on the lot and
partly on the town land; therefore the petitioners pray for an act of
assembly to have the town resurveyed, correcting any errors in the original
plot. See Arch. of Md., XLVI, 463-464. Also Calendar of Maryland State
Papers - The Black Books, p. 95.

Signers: Richard Giste, W. Hammond, Evans, William Macclein, Solomon
George Buchanan, Joseph Cromwell, Hillen, George Bailey, Jr., Thomas
John Risteau, William Rogers, John Sligh, Luke Sansbury, Nath(an)
Gill, John Bailey, Edward Reaston, Richardson, John Rattenbury, Abram
William Hopkins, William Pearce, Raven, Charles Ridgely, William
Robert Constable, John Peter Sartor, Barney, Samuel Merryman, Mathew
Abraham Hay, George Ashman, Jos(eph) Hawkins, Benjamin Knight, Thomas
Murray, Jr., Joshua Hall, Robert Harris, John Stansbury, George Eager,
North, William Fell, T. Todd, Job John Goldsmith.

BALTIMORE COUNTY LEVY PAPERS (Allowances) - 1739
J. Wells Stokes, Clerk of Court, Baltimore County. 1739 Levy papers
prepared under oath. Calendar of Maryland State Papers - The Black Books,
p. 59-60. Allowances were given to the following:

Richard Acton, Henry Adams, Benjamin Cantwell, John Cantwell, Aquila Carr,
Aderson, James Allen, Thomas Allum, James Carroll, John Casdrope, Richard
William Amass, Charles Anderson, Caswell (2), Prew Caxan, Robert
William Andrews (3), William Arnold, Chapman (2), James Chilcoate,
Anthony Asher, Walter Ashmore, John Jonathan Clasop, Dennis Coale,
Bailey, John Baily, Alexander Baker, Shipwith Coale (3), William Coale,
Charles Baker (2), Job Barns, Ford Thomas Coitly, Francis Collens,
Barus, Edmund Baxter (2), William Citturah Combest, Thomas Combest,
Bell, Joseph Bevans, Sarah Bevans, James Cooke, John Cooke (2), Sarah
Adam Birchfield, Benjamin Bond, John Cooke, Samuel Cooper, John Copeland,
Bond, Peter Bond, Richard Bond, William Copeland, Abraham Cord,
Thomas Bond, William Bond (2), Thomas Richard Coswell, Robert Courtney,
Bond (Potapsco), Thomas Bond, Jr., John Cowen, James Cranford, John
Abraham Boyd, --- Bozely, James Cranford, Ann Creagg, Samuel
Bozely, William Bozley (2), William Crockett, John Cross, Joseph Cross,
Bradford, Thomas Bradley, Thomas Richard Dallam, William Dallam,
Brerewood, Francis Brown, George Nathaniel Davice, William Davice,
Brown (Potapsco), George Browne, John Edward Day, William Deason, Richard
Browns, Anthony Brufoot, Author Deaver, Mrs. --- Debruler, William
Brumly, George Buchanan, Francis Denton, Richard Dever, William Ditto,
Buchnell, Mrs. George Buckanan, John Francis Dolohide, James Donovan,
B(uck)ingham, Jacob Bull, Selah Andrew Dorsey, Comfort Dorsey, John
Burton, Edward Bussey, Henry Butler, Dubin (2), Thomas Dulany, Stal(e)y
Richard Butts, Benjamin Cadle (2), Durham (2), Richard Eagan, Aabraham
Roger Cannon, Robert Cantable, Edward Eaglestone, John Edwards, Anthony
Enloes, John Ensor (2), Sarah Evans,
George Eves, Gregory Farmer, Gregory

31

Farmer, Jr, John Farmer, Bazalale Foster, James Fowler (2), Samuel Fowler, Thomas Franklin, Francis Freeman, Perrigrine Frisby (2), Henry Fuller, John Fuller, William Gad, James Gallion, William Galloway (2), Richard Gardner, William Garland, George Garretson (2), James Garretson, --- Garrett, William Gassaway, Joshua George, Mary Gilbert, Samuel Gilbert, Thomas Gilbort, Cassandara Giles, John Gill, Capt. Richard Gist, Christopher Gist (2), Richard Gist(4), John Gorsuch (2), Nicholas Gorsuch, Peter Gosnell, William Gosnell, Richard Gott, William Grafton, Francis Gray, William Green, James Greer, John Greer, William Grendfield, James Griffin, Samuel Griffin, Thomas Groswick, James Haddington, Frances Haile, George Hale, Edward Hall, John Hall (2), Joshua Hall (3), Parker Hall (3), Francis Hamby, Jr., Jonathan Hanson, Sarah Hanson, Elizabeth Hardiman, Loyd Harris, Thomas Harrupp, John Harryman, Samuel Harryman, William Harvey, John Hawkins, Mathew Hawkins, Thomas Hawkins, Sollomunn Hellen, Mabry Helmes, Peter Herringstraw, Henry Hicks (2), William Hitchcock, Francis Holland, George Hollingsworth, William Hollis, John Holloway (2), --- Hooke(?), Samuel Hooker (2), John Hooper, William Hopkins, Nicholas Horner, Cornelius Howard, Jonathan Howell, John Huggins, Mary Hughes, William Hughes (2), William Hunter (2), Peasly Ingram, Richard Ireland, Jacob Jackson (2), John Jackson, William Jamerson, Michael James, William James, Abraham Jarrald, William Jenkins (2), Thomas Jennings, Richard Johns, Joseph Johnson (Dear Creek), Thomas Johnson, Thomas Johnson (Dear Creek), Thomas Johnson (Fork), William Johnson, Dina Jones, Phillip Jones, Thomas Kemp, Robert Kimble, Rowland Kimble, William Knight, Dutton Lane, John Lawson, Joseph Lee, Alexander Lemmon, Ann

Lester, George Lester, Henry Lewis, Thomas Litten, William Lloyd, Thomas Lomax, Benjamin Loney, John Long, James Low, William Low, William Lowe (2), Patrick Lynch (2), Alexander Maccomas, Ann Maccomas, Ann Maccomus, Daniel Maccomus, Zacharah Mackubin, Samuel MackWilliams, Samuel Marrady, Samuel Marryman, Roger Mathews, Samuel Maxwell, William McLoud, John Medcalf, Charles Merryman, John Merryman (2), John Merryman, Jr, Josias Middlemore, Bartholomew Milhaus, Richard Mitchell (Sputia), Thomas Mitchell (Sputia), John Moale, James Moore, William Moore, Henry Morgan, Richard Morris, John Moulton, Josephus Murray, Sarah Murray, John Narwell, Benjamin Norris, Edward Norris, Joseph Norris, Thomas Norris (Forrest), Edward Norwood, Benjamin Orsbrown, William Orsbrown, (Richard) Owings, Henry Owings, John Owings, Samuel Owings, Henry Oyston, Aquila Paca (3), John Paca, Matha Paca, Richard Perkins, Richard Perkins, Jr, Joseph Perry, James Phillips, Thomas Phillips, Jonathan Plowman, Nathaniel Porter, Lewis Potee, John Poteet, William Poteet, George Presbury (3), James Preston, Mordecia Price, Robert Price, John Henry Pritchard, Obidiah Pritchard, George Purchace, Samuel Owings, Daniel Ragan, Christopher Randall, John Rattenbury, Abraham Raven, Isaac Raven, Luke Raven, Daniel Rawlings, Richard Rhoads, William Richards, Nathan Richardson, Richard Richardson, Thomas Richardson (2), Charles Ridgley, George Rigdon, George Rigdon, Jr, John Ringfield, John Risteau, John Roberts, John Roberts (Joppa) (3), John Roberts als. Camble, Thomas Francis Roberts, Charles Robinson (2), William Robinson (Gunpowder), Charles Rockhold, John Rockhold, William Rogers, Elizabeth Rove, Jacob Rowles, Daniel Ruff, Richard Ruff, Edward Rumney, Michael Rutgledge, John Rutledge, Thomas Rutter, Richard Sampson (2), Edward Sanders, Daniel

Scott, Daniel Scott, Jr., Robert
Scott, Bever Shane, John Sharp, ---
Sheredine, Thomas Sheredine,
Priscilla Simkins, Thomas Sligh (2),
Edward Smeeting, Elizabeth Smith,
Zachariah Smith, Mary Smith (Delph),
Samuel Smith (Potapsco), Edward
Sprucebanks, John Standford,
(Belsome) Standiford, James
Standiford, William Standiford (4),
John Stansbury (2), Luke Stansbury,
Thomas Stansbury, Thomas Stansbury,
Jr, --- Stansbury, Sr., John Starkey,
Joshua Starkey, Giles Stephens, John
Stephenson, Edward Stevenson, Henry
Stevenson, John Stinchcomb, George
Stokes, Humphry Wells Stokes, J.
Wells Stokes, John Sumner (2), John
Swinard, Charles Symmonds, George
Symmonds, Edmund Talbott, William
Talbott, Abraham Taylor, Elizabeth
Taylor, John Taylor, John Taylor

(North Gunpowder), John Taylor
(Pot's), Andrew Thompson, David
Thomas, Edward Throp(e) (2), Thomas
Tipton, Walter Tolley, William
Towson, Luke Trotton, Seaborn Tucker,
Edward Tully, Sarah Turbell, John
Tye, Abraham Vaughan (2), Samuel
Vaugon, Edward Wakeman, William
Wanford, Joseph Ward (3), James
Watkins, John Watts, Isaac Webster,
John Webster (2), Michael Webster,
Samuel Webster, James Welch, Richard
Wells, Thomas Wells, John West,
Robert West, Mary Westwood, Henry
Whayland, Benjamin Wheeler, Thomas
Wheeler, John White (2), Abraham
Whiteacre, Charles Whiteacre, Luke
Wiley (2), William Wiley, Thomas
Williamson (2), John Wilson, Isaac
Wood, Joshua Wood, William
Worthington, Jacob Wright, Joseph
Wright, Thomas Wright, Joseph Yates.

Tobacco Delivered to John Crockett, circa 1716/7 (?)

Undated list from Baltimore County Land Records, Liber TR# A, pp.
524-525, (probably c. 1716/7) of persons who delivered tobacco to John
Crockett. The following persons seem to have delivered their tobacco to
George Nelson, who in turn delivered it to Crockett. (From copies held by
Richard B. Miller of Pasadena, California, edited by Robert W. Barnes.)

William Bond's note for 540
Capt. Dallahide, 765
William Noble, 448 and 3/4
Wm. Hitchens (Hutchens?), 351
Thomas Bond, 375 1/2
Coll. Maxwell, 3004
John Webster, 571
Jeremy Hakes, 216
Robert Cutchen, 1056
Thomas Hutchins, 369
John Norrington, 430
John Gallion, 756
Thomas Collins, 216
Robt. Jackson, 649
John Hammonds and John Webster, 864
Charles Simmons, 792
William Maccomas, 216
John Roberts, 342
Sarah Day, 432
William Robonson, 378

Arch'd Bolls (Rollo?), 216
Charles Herrington 688.3/4
Wm. Pickett, 626 1/2
Thomas Norris, 499
William Smith 136 3/4
Robert West, 303
John Millos, 170
John Rawling, 505
John Massey, 324
George Frezland (Freeland?), 540
Thomas Barton, 292
John Bond, 540
Nicholas Day, 324
George Yorke, 378
William Amoss, 452
Abraham Taylor, 216
John Taylor, 337.3/4
James Durham, 162
Peter Carroll 292 1/4
Gregory Farmer, 241

Tobacco Delivered to John Crockett, circa 1716/7 (?)

Thomas Litton, 196 1/2
Edw. Mead,, 302
"for rents to Henry Darnall, and done by virtue of Darnall's order, to
discharge them for 7 1/2 years rent due to Lady Baltimore, and 1 1/2 years
of rent due to present Lord Baltimore."

CATTLE AND HOG MARKS

Cattle and hog marks registered in Baltimore County Land records, copied by
Dr. Richard B. Miller of Pasadena, California, and edited by Robert Barnes.

Liber TR # 28, pp. 93-94:

John Elliott, 21 Jan. 1719   Mr. Talbott, same day
Prichard Preston, 21 Jan. 1719   Jacob Cox, 3 June 1719
Thomas Tolley, 10 Dec. 1719   John Poteet, 6 June 1719
Edward Hall, same day   Edmund Norwood, 29 Sept. 1719
Luke Trotten, same day

Liber IS#G:

p. 3 - William Hitchcock, c. 1721; Maurice Baker, c. 1721; Robert Robertson,
c. 1721
p. 5 - Henry Hicks, c. 1722
p. 33 - Araan Fox, 4 Sept. 1722
p. 36 - Jane Hattenpenny, c. 1722
p. 37 - Eliz. Whitehead, c. 1722; Skelton Standifer, c. 1722
p. 57 - James Maxwell, eld. son of Col. James Maxwell, Jan. 1722; John
Stokes, c. 1722
p. 60 - Phoebe Whitehead, c. 1720-2; Frances or Francis Whitehead, c.
1720-2; Charles Smith, c. 1722; Thomas Johnson; Robert Whitehead
p. 61 - Thomas Hutchins; Thos. Rider
p. 74 - Thomas Bayley, c. 1722
p. 108 - William Wrise, 1 May 1723; Col. John Dorsey
p. 139 - William Rogers, 1 March 1722; Thomas Bayley; James Little; Walter
James, 1 May 1723
p. 140 - Benjamin Norris, 1 March 1722; John Nelson; Hannah Nelson (at
request of John Nelson; William Hughes, March 1721

Liber IS#G:

p. 140 - Luke Raven, Sr., 7 March 1721; Wm. Deadford, 6 March 1722; John
Ensor, 20 April 1723; Wm. Enloes, same day; John Durbin, 1 March
p. 141 - Thomas Sheredine, 16 April 1723; Avanto Phelps, 17 April 1723 (at
request of father Thomas Phelps); Alexander Crouch(?), Nov. 1722; Job
Barnes, 30 March 1723
p. 143 - John Smithers, 28 May 1723
p. 144 - James Rider, 6 June 1723; John Roberts of S. side Gunpowder R., 3
July 1724
P. 151 - Martha Devans, dau. of John and Mary, 10 July 1723; Thomas
Giddings, 7 July 1723; Richard Robinson, 10 July 1723
p. 152 - John Cooper, 30 July; Humphrey Yates, 20 June; Wm. Reves, 20 June;
James Rider, 20 June; Robert Lusby, 20 June; Lloyd Harris, 1 June

CATTLE AND HOG MARKS

p. 158 - Richard ..., Aug. 1723; Robert ...; Jonathan ..., 3 Sept. 1723;
Henry Wetheral, 3 Sept. 1723
p. 231 - Isaac Webster, 4 March 1723; Jacob Morris, 18 March; Samuel Durham,
18 March; John Maccomas, 18 March
p. 242 - James Moore, shoemaker; 20 March 1723
p. 249 - Richard Deaver
p. 258 - Henry Enloes, 30 May 1724; John Huggins, same; Isaac Webster, same
p. 266 - James Padgett, 25 June 1724
p. 288 - Anthony Asher, 9 Aug. 1724; Thomas Cord, same; Thomas Shy(?), 1
Sept. 1724
p. 303 - William Brazier, 15 Nov. 1724; Patrick Ruark, 16 Nov.; John
Roberts, tailor, 10 Oct; James Hanford (or Stanford), 14 Oct.; Wm. Right, 15
Oct.; Samuel Stansbury, 5 June; Aquila Hall, 6 June; John Gallaher, 7 June;
Cornelius Poulson, 8 June; James Fugatt, 9 June; Joseph Allen, 6 Aug.; John
Debruler, 11 Aug.

List of debts dated 16 June 1720: Richard Bennett and Thomas Bordley, Esq.;
assignments for debts to be paid ... contracted by Mr. Francis Sutton for
use of the estate of Wm. Matthew Esq., Balto. Co. Land Records, TR#DS, p.
175, abstracted by Dr. Richard B. Miller.

Mr. Francis Holland, 1832
Mr. William Marshall, 984
Robert Clark for building, 600
Wm. Lowery for cow and calf, 500
Mr. Richard King, for goods, 500
James Paul for taylor's work, 1250
Samuel Jackson for 2 cows and calves, 1400
Dr. Middlemore's acct. so much as taken up for the servant plantation's use
...
Wm. Cotton, for shoe, 200
Benj. Brown, for building, 500
George Eves, due of his crop but to allow for one cross cut saw and ox chain
saw, 600
John Bailey for smith work, 100
Mr. Edward Hall, 3268
John Ryon, 460

Taken from Balto. Co. Deeds, Liber TR # DS, p. 116, abstracted by Dr.
Richard B. Miller:
11 August 1720 - Thomas Wilson and Rich. Gresham came into court and proved
the following power of attorney was granted by John Willis on 14 April 1720
to Capt. Stephen Yoakley, commander of the ship Mary, now bound for
Maryland, to collect the following debts, witnessed by said Wilson and
Richard Gresham before Jacobus Dunindge, Not. Publ.:
Thomas Cromwell, 19.16.6 1/2
Bennett Garrett 6.14.3 1/4
Henry Hendrickson 6.14.11
Samuel Norris 2.12.6 3/4
Peter Numbers 1.9.19 1/2
Joseph Johnson 2.12.9 1/2

LIST OF DEBTS

Nich's Rogers 14.8.9 1/2
Joseph Presbury 6.13.3
Jabez Pierpoint 2.7.5
Wm. Wheream 7.3.4 1/2
John Buck 5.11.11 3/4
James Isham 3.9.4
John Flemming 1.13.6
Richard Burroughs 17.19.1
Anthony Bale 7.19.4 1/2
Edwd. Skidmore 13.5.7 3/4
Nich. Fitsimonds 62.11.10 3/4
Jane Gill 1.14.1
John Hurst 10.17.6 1/4
Peter Bond, exec. of Hill Savage
21.10.6 3/4
John Martin 9.5.7
Wm. Cox 119.17.3 1/2
Thomas Randall 3.19.4 1/2
John Grisham 1.5.7 1/2

4 August 1722 - The following servants were convicted for the stated crime for 7 years, from the City of Exon, in the Reformation, /s/ Philip Weare, commander (Recorded in Balto. Co. Deeds, Liber IS#G, p. 34, abstracted by Richard B. Miller.)
John Lux, for robbing a woman
William Camp, for house robbing
Thomas Camp for house robbing
John James, for robbing his landlady
Wm. Gater, for house stealing
John Brisk, for stealing a coat
Thomas Hill, for stealing a bag of small things
Nich. Commins, for stealing of wine
Wm. Berriman for forcing a maid
Martha Whyett for stocking a maid
Elizabeth Quick for stealing two head cloths
Sarah Griffith, for stealing 2 handkerchiefs

Old Indian Road, Baltimore County
Printed in William B. Marye's article on "The Old Indian Road," Md. Hist. Magazine, 15: 220-221 (June, 1920). Taken from Liber HWS # IA # 2, 1736-1738, folios 311 and 356.

In November 1738, Joseph Murray presented a petition to the County Court, stating that "Whereas some person or persons by his or their contrivance have obtained an order of the Court to clear the old Indian Road through a fine meadow of your petitioner ..." he asks permission of the court to turn the said road, and the following persons signed, as being content with Murray's turning the said road. (Notes in parentheses following each name refer to the land owned by that individual according to the 1750 Debt Book.)

Cornelius Howard (In 1750 Debt Book, owned: pt Cornelius and Mary's Lot, 100 a.; Joshua's Gift, 57 a.; Howard's Square, 150 a.; and other.)

William Gist (In 1750 Debt book, owned: Woolf Den, 50 a.; Gits's Enlarge-
ment, 50 a.; The Addition, 60 a.)
Joshua Howard (Not listed in 1750 Debt Book)
John Hawkins (In 1750 Debt Book, owned: pt Mount Organ and Simkins Repose,
160 a.; and Isingley's Glade, 44 a.)
Samuel Owings (In 1750 Debt Book, owned: pt Green Spring Punch, 286 a.;
Addition, 150 a.; Severn, 100 a.; Come By Chance, 50 a.; Rich Meadow, 100
a.)
George Ashman (In 1750 Debt Book, owned pt Counterscarpe, 134 a.; Addition
to Counterscarpe, 20 a.; Ashman's Delight, 230 a.
Thomas Wells (1750 Debt Book showed Thomas Wells, Jr., as owning: Thomas
Adventure, 50 a.; Wells Meadow, 50 a.; Hollow Rock, 100 a.; Jacob's Well,
50 a.)
Thomas Gist (In 1750 Debt Book, owned: pt The Adventure, 216 a.)
Nathaniel Gist (Not in 1750 Debt Book)
William Lewis (In 1750 Debt Book, owned: pt Cornelius and Mary's Lot, 100
a.; Howards Fancy, 200 a.; pt The Reserve, 100 a.; The Friendship, 100
a.)
Edmond Howard (Not in 1750 Debt Book)
Matthew Coulter (Not in 1750 Debt Book)
Lawrence Hammond (Not in 1750 Debt Book)
John Wooley of Connaagee (Not in 1750 Debt Book - ?)
John Dirumple (Not in 1750 Debt Book)
Charles Motherby (In 1750 Debt Book, owned: pt Mount Organ, 250 a.;
Motherby's Adventure, 50 a.)
John Simkin (In 1750 Debt Book, owned: pt Organ and Simkin's Addition, 40
a.; Simkin's Repose, 100 a.)
Charles Hissey (In 1750 Debt Book, owned: Young's Chance, 18 a.)
George Bailey (In 1750 Debt Book, owned: pt Athol, 217 a.; Baileys
Inheritance, 323 a.; The Hopeyard, 100 a.)
Thomas Brothers (In 1750 Debt Book, owned: Stevensons Plains, 100 a.
Anthony Brayfoot (Not listed in 1750 Debt Book)
James Wells (In 1750 Debt Book, owned: Rogue's Ridge, 100 a.
Christopher Gist (Not listed in 1750 Debt Book)

In 1738 another petition was sent into the County Court, asking the same
thing as the earlier one. This one was signed by the following:
Samuel Owings (See above)
Christopher Gist (See above)
Thomas Gist (See above)
Richard Pinkham (In 1750 Debt Book, owned: pt Matthews Forest, 50 a.
Edward Roberts (Not listed in 1750 Debt Book)
Peter Magers (Not listed in 1750 Debt Book)
John Cook (In 1750 Debt Book reference is made to the heirs of John Cook who
owned pt Maiden Mount, 50 a.; pt Paradice, 50 a. and also to a John Cook
who owned Welches Adventure, 200 a.)
Edward Reeston (In 1750 Debt Book, owned: Turkey Cock Hall, 200 a.)
John Cockey (Not listed in 1750 Debt Book)
James Chilcoate (Not listed in 1750 Debt Book)
John Hawkins (See above)
James Wells (See above)
William Lewis (See above)

OLD INDIAN ROAD

Richard Jones (Not listed in 1750 Debt Book)
James Wells (In 1750 Debt Book, owned: Hickory Bottom, 50 a.; and James'
    Fancy)
Thomas Wells (In 1750 Debt Book there is a listing for a Thomas Wells, Jr,
    who owned: Thomas' Adventure, 50 a.; Wells Meadow, 50 a.; Hollow Rock,
    100 a.; Jacobs Well, 50 a.)
John Dorumple, Jr. (Not listed in 1750 Debt Book)
John Medcalf (Not listed in 1750 Debt Book)
George Bailey (See above)
Mathew Coulter (See above)
Charles Motherby (See above)
Cornelius Howard (See above)
John Simkin (See above)
William Seabrook (In 1750 Debt Book, owned: Taylors Farm, 100 a.; London, 50
    a.)
Joseph Cromwell (In 1750 Debt Book, owned: Deirk Park, 220 a.; Cromwell's
    Enlargement, 260 a.)
Thomas Bond (In 1750 Debt Book, Thomas Bond of Peter owned pt Logsdons
    Addition, 32 1/2 a.; pt Bedford Resurveyed, 140 a.; Bonds Forest, 27 a.;
    Wooleys Range, 100 a.; Bonds Meadows, 100 a.)
Josephus Murray (In 1750 Debt Book, owned: Elleges Farm, 50 a.; Murrays
    Plains, 300 a.; Murrays Farm, 100 a.)

From Historical Sketches of St. Paul's Parish in Baltimore County, Maryland
by The Rev. Ethan Ellen. Baltimore, 1855. Unpublished. Contributors to
the building the first place of public worship in Baltimore Town. Besides
the assessments ordered by the assembly on the parish for building the new
church there were also individual subscriptions for this purpose. Those
mentioned in the Treasurer's book are: George Bailey, Geo. Buchanan, Wm.
Buckner, John Cromwell, Joseph Cromwell, Walter Dallas, Charles Dorsey, R.
Gist, William Hammond, Lloyd Harris, Francis Hinkley, Joshua Howard, Hyde
Hoxton, Elizabeth Huett, Richard Lewis, John Moale, George Ogg, John
Parrish, Christopher Randall, Christopher Randall, Jr., David Reister, John
Restian(?), Edw. Riester., Jonas Robinson, William Rodgers, John Simkin,
John Townshend, George Walker, John Wooley

Lot Owners in Old Joppa at the time of its establishment.
Courthouse (?); Joseph Calvert "late merchant of Kent County;" Joseph
Calvert (3 lots); John Crockett; Nicholas Day; Greenbury Dorsey (son of Col.
John Dorsey); John Hall, Jr. - later Samuel Ward, Carpenter; William Hammond
- later Nicholas Day; Richard Hewitt; Catherine Hollingsworth, widow;
Catherine Hollingsworth for son Valentine Hollingsworth; Daniel Hughes -
later Jonathan Hughes; James Isham (3 lots); Benjamin Jones - Jeremiah
Sutton; William Lowe (2 lots); Samuel Maccubins; Roger Matthews; Col. James
Maxwell; Aquilla Paca - later William Lowe; Aquila Paca (sheriff of the
county); John Roberts; Capt. Thomas Sheredine; John Stokes; Thomas Tolley;
Joseph Ward, inn-holder - later Nicholas Day; Thomas White Clerk of the
Court

LEASES FOR THREE LIFE TIMES

Individuals renting lands from Lord Baltimore's land agents often rented the land for three life times. The related document specified the family members by name and usually their ages. The following names and ages, with the dates of the lease, are taken from Baltimore County Land Records.

Liber HWS # 1-A

p. 66 - 30 Sep 1736: George Elliott, Ann Elliott, and Susanna Westwood (ages and relationships not given).

p. 72 - 10 Dec 1737: Daniel Shaw, wife Eliz. Shaw, and William Hall, son of Thomas and Ann Hall.

p. 118 - 10 June 1738: Ralph Bradack, wife Elizabeth, and their dau Ann Bradack.

p. 166 - 10 Dec 1736: James Standiford, wife Martha, and dau Chloe.

p. 327 - 24 July 1739: Thomas Burk, wife Sarah, Richard Burk (son of Ulic Burk who was the father of said Thomas).

p. 367 - 2 Nov 1739: William Low, John Low, and Thomas Low.

p. 371 - 2 Nov 1739: Israel Johnson, Melchisedek Johnson, and Nathan Johnson, all sons of Thomas Johnson.

p. 390 - 2 Mar 1737: Susannah, Thomas, and James Gittings, children of Thomas Gittings.

p. 399 - 28 Feb 1739: James Crow, Hannah Crow, and Ruth Beliken.

p. 428 - 5 June 1740: William Dallam, wife Elizabeth, and son Jonas.

p. 536 - 7 Aug 1741: Edward Mortimore, wife Eleanor, and Esther Bray, dau of Eleanor.

Liber TB # A

p. 218 - 24 July 1742: William Rowe, c.38; son William, Jr., c.6; dau Ann, 8.

Liber TB # C

p. 21 - 15 Nov 1740: Daniel Pocock, for lives of Susannah Pocock, 50; son John, c.14; and son Able, c.7.

p. 24 - 8 July 1742: Luke Wiley, c.36; Luke, Jr., c.3; and son Walter, c.3 months.

p. 27 - 25 Oct 1742: Francis Hines, c.35; wife Frances, c.23; son Samuel, c.2

p. 52 - 15 Oct 1742: Thomas Marshall, c.34; wife Sarah, c.22; son John, c.1.

p. 55 - 15 Oct 1742: Martin Bacon, c.26; wife Mary, c.22; and her son William Watson, c.5.

p. 79 - 13 Nov 1742: Walter Carr of Calvert Co., merchant, c.46; son Walter, Jr., c.8; son Seaborn, c.10.

p. 82 - 25 Nov 1742: Jacob Frizell, of Anne Arundel Co., c.21; Abraham, Jr., c.20; and Ann Taylor, c.16.

p. 85 - 25 Nov 1742: Nathaniel Sheapard, c.70; wife Eliz., c.50; son John (by wife Elizabeth), c.30.

p. 106 - 15 Nov 1740: John Shewbridge, for lives of son John, c.2; dau Elizabeth, c.7; dau Mary, c.5.

p. 108 - 25 Nov 1742: James Fugate, c.66; son James alias Peter, c.15; son James, c.13.

p. 111 - 25 Oct 1742: William Watkins, c.22; wife Ann, c.22; bro. John, c.15.

LEASES FOR THREE LIFE TIMES

p. 115 – 25 Nov 1742: John Huggins, Jr., 22; wife Mary. c.17; bro. Daniel, c.9.

p. 118 – 25 Nov 1742: Thomas Anderson, c.41; William Wiley of Luke, c.10; and Benj. Anderson of Benj., c.11.

p. 121 – 14 Dec 1742: Jacob Bull, for lives of son Isaac, c.15; son Samuel, c.17; son Edmund, c.13

p. 124 – 16 Feb 1742: Benjamin Anderson, c.33; wife Sarah, c.35; son William, c.14.

p. 127 – 25 Nov 1742: Moses Collett, c.24; Daniel Collett, c.18; William Anderson, c.14.

p. 130 – 25 Nov 1742: Peter Knowles, c.26; wife Mary, c.19; son Peter, c. 1.

p. 133 – 16 Feb 1742: John Sharp, c.29; wife Eliz., c.32; Nathaniel Sheapard of William, c.10.

p. 135 – 22 Feb 1742: Thomas Oakley, c.30; wife Prudence, c.27; son Thomas, Jr., c.1.

p. 138 – 25 Nov 1742: John Frizell of A.A. Co. for lives of son Gale, c.19; son Nathan, c.12; dau Susanna, c.15.

p. 141 – 25 Nov 1742: Charles Prosser for lives of wife Mary, c.30; dau Eliz., c.4; dau Sarah, c.2.

p. 146 – 25 Jan 1742: John Armstrong, c.61; wife Rebena, c.43; son Henry, c.23

p. 149 – 25 Nov 1742: James Marsh, c.34; wife Margaret, c.23; son James, c.4.

p. 151 – 15 Feb 1742: Henry Taylor, c.32; Luke Wiley of Luke, c.3; Martha Wiley of Luke, c.12.

p. 154 – 25 Nov 1742: Edmund Deason, c.22; wife Eliz., c.17; dau Rebecca, c.2 months.

p. 156 – 25 Nov 1742: Samuel Deason for lives of son William, c.5; dau Jemima, c.2; twin dau Mary, c.2.

p. 159 – 16 Feb 1742: William Armstrong, c.27; wife Eliz., c.26; dau Temperance, c.6.

p. 199 – 11 Dec 1742: William Slade, c.26; wife Eliz., c.20; dau Margaret, c.2.

p. ... – 30 Mar 1743: John Wiley, for lives of John, Jr., c.15; son Benj., c.7; son Able, c.5 (page is between 201 and 206).

p. 206 – 25 Nov 1742: Edward Mortemore, c.38; wife Eleanor, c.39; Hester Bray, c.18

p. 209 – 11 Dec 1742: Thomas Slade of A.A. Co., c.25; Ann Besson, c.18; Margaret, c.1.

p. 211 – 22 Feb 1742: William Wright, c.26; wife Sarah, c.23; dau Mary, 4 months.

p. 228 – 25 Apr 1743: Michael Connoley, c.39; son Henry (?), c.5; dau Bridget, c.3.

p. 231 – 12 Apr 1743: William Hunt, c.33; wife Eliz., c.24; dau Sarah, c.4.

p. 233 – 21 Apr 1743: John Fuller (of Thomas), c.28; wife Ruth, c.25; son Thomas, c.3.

p. 235 – 27 Apr 1743: John Huggins, Sr., c.43; son John, Jr., c.21; son William, c.12.

p. 284 – 15 July 1743: John Grimes, c.36; wife Mary, c.35; dau Mary, c.8.

p. 371 – 16 Jun 1743: Nehemiah Hicks, for lives of sons Isaac, Nehemiah, and Jacob – ages not given.

p. 392 – 16 Nov 1743: John Low, Thos. Low, William Low (ages not given).

LEASES FOR THREE LIFE TIMES

p. 418 — 16 Nov 1743: Jacob, Aaron, and Luke Johnson (ages and relationships not given, but Jacob is called son of Thomas).

p. 431 — 15 Nov 1743: John Tyler, c.44; dau Tirla(?), 6; dau Eliza, 4.

p. 433 — 15 Nov 1743: Jonathan Ady, c.24; wife Rebecca, c.17; dau Rachel, 14 days.

p. 436 — 15 Nov 1743: Thomas Willmouth, c.31; son Thomas, c.4; dau Mary, c.2.

p. 438 — 15 Nov 1743: John Spencely, c.24; wife Jane, c.24; dau Eliza, 6 weeks.

p. 440 — 15 Dec 1743: John Hooper, c.44; Mary Fugate now Mary Knowles, c.20; Ann Fugate's dau Jane, c.7.

p. 443 — 18 Jan 1743: Gale Frizzell, for lives of wife Susanna, c.20; John, Jr., son of John Frizzell, Sr., 18; and Wm. Blizard, son of Elizabeth, c.12.

p. 445 — 20 Jan 1743: Edward Mortemore, c.38; wife Elenor, c.39; Hester Bray, c.18.

p. 447 — 10 Feb 1743: James Maydwell, c.29; Eliz. Ady Garrison, c.22; her son Job Garriscn, c.2.

p. 450 — 15 Feb 1743: Daniel Pocock, c.53; son John, c.17; son Abell, c.10.

p. 452 — 16 Feb 1743: Israel Standiford, c.23; wife Cassandra, c.17; Benjamin Anderson, c.17.

p. 457 — 16 Nov 1743: John Standiford, Skelton Standiford, and William Standiford (ages and relationships not stated).

p. 460 — 16 Nov 1743: Aquila Greer, Eliz. Greer, and Sarah Greer (ages and relationships not given).

p. 488 — 24 Apr 1744: William Row, c.40; son William, Jr., c.8; dau Ann, c.10.

p. 492 — 12 Apr 1744: Charles Prosser; wife Mary, c.31; dau Eliza, c.5; dau Sarah, c.3.

p. 496 — 12 Apr 1744: William Wright, c.27; wife Sarah, c.24; dau Mary c.19 months.

p. 499 — 20 Apr 1744: John Bull, c.28; John Bacon son of Martin, 1; Eliz. Bacon, 3.

p. 502 — 12 Apr 1744: John Bourne, c.28; dau Mary Davis, c.23; John Anderson, c.4.

p. 505 — 12 Apr 1744: Edward Haley/Hailey, c.37; dau Mary c.5; dau Ann, c.4.

p. 509 — 12 Apr 1744: John Spencely, c.24; wife Jane, c.24; dau Eliz., c.6 months.

p. 516 — 12 Apr 1744: John Barton, c.29; wife Ann, c.20; dau Jamima, c.16 (sic).

p. 552 — 30 Dec 1743: John Fuller of Thomas, c.29; wife Ruth, c.26; son Thomas, 4.

p. 556 — 1 May 1744: Francis Hines, c.39; w. Frances, 23; son Samuel, c.4.

p. 559 — 28 May 1744: Thomas Hamilton, c.50; son Thomas, Jr., c.14; dau Margaret, c.17.

p. 583 — 21 Aug 1744: Paul Garron, c.35; son John, c.12; son James, c.9.

p. 587 — 1 Sep 1744: William Harman, c.36; wife Sarah, c.30; her son Edward Powell, c.3.

p. 590 — 1 Sep 1744: Thomas Slade, c.26; Ann Beeson of A.A. Co, c.19; Mary Slade, c.2.

p. 593 — 3 Sep 1744: William Bull, c.25; wife Martha, c.24; dau Eleanor, c.3.

p. 596 - 10 Sep 1744: Benj. Coale, c.29; wife Margaret, c.25; son Benjamin, Jr., c.one-half year.

p. 598 - 12 Sep 1744: Paul Garron, c.25 (35?); son John, c.12; son James, c.9.

p. 601 - 20 Sep 1744: William Carson, c.24; wife Eliz., c.16; her bro. Andrew Johnson, c.8.

p. 603 - 20 Sep 1744: Thomas Oakley, c.30; wife Prudence, c.28; son Thomas, Jr., c.2.

p. 606 - 20 Sep 1744: Nicholas Seavers, c.38; Eliza, c.33; Nicholas, Jr., c.1.

p. 610 - 20 Sep 1744: John Wood, tailor, c.50; wife Ann, c.44; Charles Seavers of Nicholas, c.9.

p. 613 - 20 Sep 1744: Thomas Hamilton, c.50; son Thomas, Jr., c.14; dau Margaret, c.17.

p. 616 - 25 Sep 1744: Nicholas Seavers, c.38; John Wood, c.50; Eliz. Seavers, c.33; Lidia Seavers, c.10; Prudence Seavers, c.5; Ann Wood, c.44.

p. 620 - 1 Oct 1744: Thomas Fisher, c.34; Martha Harding, c.24; Martha Terry, c.40.

p. 623 - 5 Oct 1744: John Rockhold, c.33; son Jacob, c.4; son John, Jr., c.2.

Liber TB # D
p. 71 - 25 Feb 1744/5: William Standiford; wife Christiana; son Aquila (ages not given)

p. 165 - 20 Apr 1745: Peter (sic) Garron, c.40; son James, c.3 months; dau Mary, c.5.

p. 176 - 20 Dec 1744: Edward Haley, c.38; dau Mary, c.6; dau Ann, c.?

p. 180 - 1 Oct 1744: Robert Whitehead, c.45; w. Eliza, c.4-?; son Thomas, c.4.

p. 189 - June 1745: Samuel Thornhill, c.40; John Boring (Marshall?), son of Thomas Marshall, c.21; Eliza Prosser, dau of Charles, c.-?

p. 194 - Dec 1744: William Wright, c.-8?; wife Sarah, c.--?; dau ---, c. 2.

p. 217 - 10 Dec 1745: Samuel Talbie, c.35; w. Eliza, c.23; son Zepheniah, c.3.

p. 221 - 2 Jan 1744: Andrew Knowland, c.27; wife Margaret, c.23; dau Frances, c.3.

p. 225 - 30 Jan 1744: John Hooper, c.45; Mary Fugate now Knowles, c.21; Ann Fugate, dau of James, c.8.

p. 230 - 24 Sep 1744: Thomas Franklin, James Franklin, and James Ingram (ages and relationships not given).

p. 340 - 17 Sep 1745: William Harvey, Margrett Harvey, and Thomas Harvey (ages and relationships not given).

p. 425 - 17 Sep 1745: Henry Hicks, James Hicks, Laban Hicks, and Henry Hicks (last three are sons of the first Henry Hicks).

Liber TB # E
p. 95 - 17 July 1746: John Hatton, wife Sarah
p. 352 - 10 Oct 1746: Jonathan Ady, c.27; son William, c.14 (sic); wife Rebecca, c.22.
p. 356 - same day: Jonathan Ady, c.27; wife Rebecca, c.22; dau Rachel, c.3.

LEASES FOR THREE LIFE TIMES

p. 360 – 26 May 1744: Charles Cole, c.22; bro. Joseph, c.18; bro. Matthew, c.12.

p. 362 – 10 June 1745: Cornelius Stewart, c.41; Arthur Brownlee, Jr., c.10; Joseph Brownlee, c.7.

p. 365 – 15 Feb 1744: Thomas Beamsley, c.40; Mary Beamsley, c.32; Sarah Deason, c.4, dau of Samuel.

p. 368 – 1 Sep 1746: John Crockett, c.30; wife Ann, c.30; Ann Row, c.8, dau of William.

p. 371 – 10 Mar 1745: John Christeson, c.22; wife Margaret, c.19; Thomas Hamilton, c.16. (John Christian married Margaret Hamilton on 12 Sep 1743: St. Johns Parish, p. 193.)

p. 390 – 7 Apr 1747: Stephen Scarlett, wife Ruth Scarlett (ages not given).

ALIENATION FEES

A list, dated 1734, of alienation fees paid to Humphrey Wells Stokes for Samuel Chew and Philip Thomas. Taken from Baltimore County Land Records, Liber HWS # M, p. 173, abstracted by Dr. Richard B. Miller of Pasadena, California.

18 May Richard Snowden to Joshua Starkey – Colenbourne, 200 a.

5 June Thomas Cross to William Hughes – pt Hughes Chance, 10 a.

5 June Thomas League to William Rhodes – pt Hughes Chance, 50 a.

6 June John White to Seaborn Tucker – Batchelders Beginning, 100a.

6 June John Lowe to John White – pt Paradice, 50 a.

5 June Antil Deaver to Nathan Rigbie – 1/2 of Parker's Chance, 275 a.

7 June John White to Nathan Rigbie – pt Paradice, 50a.

8 Aug Jacob Giles and Isaac Webster to Job Barnes – pt Brothers Discovery, 50a.

9 Aug Henry Rhodes to John Nelson – pt Birr, 133 1/3 a.

8 Aug William Rhodes to Theophilus Jones et uxor (and wife) – pt Hews Chance, 60 a.

10 Aug William Cannon to John Lowe – pt Paradice, 50 a.

10 Aug Isaac Grice to John Maccubbin – Chestnutt Neck, 150 a.

5 Aug Jonathan Tipton to John Chilcoat – pt Addn to Poor Jamaica Man's Plague, 30 a.

13 July Thomas Porter et ux (wife) to Wm. Rogers – Crowleys Venture, 100 a.

8 Aug Thomas Brashiers et ux (wife) to Isaac Webster – 10 a.

11 Feb Wm. Burney(?) to John Jamerson – London, 100 a.; pt Pitchcraft & pt Polecat Ridge, 100 a.

14 May Isaac Whiteacre to Aquila and John Paca – pt Whiteacres Ridge, 50 a.

8 Aug John Lowe to William Cannon, pt Paradice, 50 a.

1750 Assessor's Field Book of Baltimore County

Held by State Archives, Accession number 16,927

Only the names are listed here. Omitted are the names of tracts, number of slaves, cattle etc. in the original. In the original document the names are often mispelled; the handwriting is difficult to interpret. James is consistently spelled Jems, Caleb becomes Calep, George becomes Gorge, etc. It is significant to note that there are many names in this list that are not found in the 1754 Debt Book of Baltimore County.

A typical entry reads, "Jeremiah Biddeson - Beddesons Neck 466 at 3 - 3 male negros 20 - improvements 30 - 14 on plate 3 horses 15 - 6 cows 24 - 14 sheep 14 - house lot & furnutuure 50."

Many of the variations in spelling are obvious. When doubt might arise the compiler shows in brackets [] his suggestion as to the intended word or name.

Samuel Atherger
Gorge Alderson
William Armatge
Peter Atman
Samuel Att lives on Danel Stivrs land
Robert Elliott lives on Mrs. Chambers land
William Asher
Marcey Arriat
William H. Andres [Andrews]
Ahialitter [Aquilla?] Asher
Walter Ashe lives with his mother
Isaac Asher
Doctor Joseph Allender
Sarah Allender widow of Thoms.
Jemes Armstrong
John Baxley of Rd.(?) lives at S. Mill
Robert Button
Benjamin Bedford blac(k) man - a lot on Philadelphia Road
Philip Bowens
John Bumbargar
John Barker
Joshua Biven
Edward J. Boing [Bowen, Boring?]
Jeremiah Biddeson
Absolem Boing [Bowen, Boring?]
John Buck
Providence Baker
Joseph Bias [Biays]
James Bivins lives on John Hattens land
Nicholas Brice
one lot beling to a french man joyns [joins] Judge Brices lot
Lavin [Levin] Barray [Berry]
Cristen [Christian] Gilback

Ann Chambers a widdow
Arther Brian lives on Mrs. Partdgs land [Patridge]
Hannan Barrackman
Thomas Bond
Jemes Bond heirs
Toby Bonds heirs
Jemes Byas [Biays]
William Boley
Thomas Burgen
Jems Baker trustee for Cid Lynchs familey
Jemes Brice lives on the point pt of Darby Hall
Elinor Battee
William and Josiah Bond lives on Abram Eglesons land
James Busk heirs on J. Gersuchs [Gorsuch] land
Greenbury Busk
Ann Busk
Fredrick Brian lives on the ... land
Ephrion [Ephraim] Carback lives on John Suddens land
Arthur Cunningham lives on the land belonging to Dr. Hustar
John Bell lives on Attburgor land
Jems Coe lives on Loyd Goodings
George Counselman
Jacob Calk
Robert Conway
John Clark lives on John Owens land
Charls Carrol lives on Robert Gallows land
Thomas Carter [Contee?] heirs
William Cook
John Carback son of Jno. heirs on Daneil Mityka land

44

Hesakiah Carback lives on Mr.
  Stemmans land
John Carback
Maray Curten [Mary Curtain]
Jems Cummings blac(k) man lives on
  Batt Greens land
Jems Carrol black man lives on Mrs.
  Gallaway land
Thomas Couley on pt of the principio
  land
Maray Cartwright lives on Calep
  Goodings land
Ann Channel
William Clark
Robert Cooper lives on Ffrs.
  [Francis] Battee and Stinsbury
  [Stansbury] land
Richard Catrin [Calvin?] pt of Coluns
  land
John Carback of Thomas pt of David(?)
  Stansbury land
Thomas Carback lives on Ed. Welch
  land
Gorge Collins
Jemes Crooks
Mrs. Goldsmith widdow of Coplin
Jemes Carrol and Mrs. Gouff [Gough]
Barnet H. Cook lives at Rigtes stone
  tavern
Elisabeth Cristopher
Charls. Crook
Jemes Crisp - and Levy Howard lives
  on the land
Sam Dixon black man lives on Lynch
  Griffins land
Mikel Deal lives on William
  Weatheabys land
Cumberland Dugan pt of the principy
  Co. land
George Dublin, collerd man lives on
  Jeremiah Bedsen [Biddison] land
Charls S. Davis
John Duffey lives on Thomas Hust
  [Stuart?] land
William Dew
Fednik Dew
Jemes Duffin, collerd man
Ezikiel Davis
Arch Davis lives on Betsey Longs land
Michal Denney lives on Jems
  Stansbury land

Jemes Davis pt of Arther Cheys
  formly[?] Elisbeth Otenen
Zariah Dullom [Dallam]
Edward Darsy(?) [Dorsey'
William Dimmet (land of?) Jems
  Forrest
Henry Deal
Dorse and Idare
Roibart Dunwooddy
Abram Egleson [Eggleston]
Joshua Egleson [Eggleston] lives on
  Baleys land
John Edwards
Martin Eihelberger [Eichelberger]
Elisabeth Edwards
Robert Fitch
Earnest Calip
William Ffalts [This could be Falls
  or Felts] lives on Mr. R. Smiths
  land (all following "lives" is
  scratched out)
Benjaman Furegson [Furguson?]
William Fitch of Henry
John Fuce [Fuss]
Sarah Flax
William Fuce [Fuss]
Richard Frisby
Francis Firemans [Forman?] formerly
  Barrakman property ... the society
  of Friends pt of Huntington
William Fitch
Jacob Fuse [Fuss]
Jemes Woolf
George Ford lives on the land of
  Crook Ars [heirs]
Jems Ferel lives on Bartons old place
John Fitches
Thomas Fitchs
Joseph R. Ford
Paul A. Flenny
Loud Goodewin
Robert Green
Lynch Grifin
Joseph Grifin
William Grimes lives on Benjaman
  Green land
William Gibson
Harris Griddle lives on Robert Green
  land
Josiah Green
John Gorman lives on Abram Eglestons
  land

45

John M. Gorsuch
Rebecca Gray g(u)ardian for John
    Ashhaw(?)
Benjamin Green garden [guardian] for
    Zeriah Green
Calep Gooden
Gross and Baker
John Goodwin
Robert Gorsuch
Sarah Gregroy
Stephen Grimes
Robart C. Galloway
Ruth Gotts
Nicholas Grimes lives on Garretsons
    old place
John Gregory
John Graves
William Gilmore lives on Hoppy land
Peter Bauer Grace Bartons place
Stephen Gornby (?)
Moses Galloway
William Guyn [Gwinn]
Catherine Galloways
Mary Harraman [Harriman]
Henry Hughes lives on John Suddens
    land
Thomas Harraman lives on Doc(t)r.
    Bonds land
Soloman Hughs
John Hillin
Will. Heslip
John Heslip
William Hunt (on) Quiller [Aquilla]
    Parks land
Pompey Han lives on Mrs. Stuert land
    - black man
John Hardless
John E. Howard
Ely Hatton garden [guardian] for
    Thomas Hattens Ares [heirs]
Levy Howard Heares [heirs] on the
    Youngs land
Yestus Hoppy
Elizabeth Hencock [Hancock]
Stephen Harraman [Harriman] lives on
    John Murray land
Rebacca Hutton
Jemes Hargets
John Hughs
Jemes Hughs lives on Ruth Gots land
Enegness Hatter
David Hickman

Runyan Hames
Boript(?) Hart
Jems Ha..letton [Hasleton?,
    Hambelton?]
George Hiday
Cristoper Hughs
Isaac Hollingworth lives in Harfort
    [Harford County]
Elisabeth Hughes
Edward A. Howard
Edward A. Howard and wife Gerden
    [guardian] for John Days heirs
John B. Howard
George Hankins
Jemes Hutton
John Hatton
Jeane Jones widdow lives on Worthings
    land
Sam Jones black man lives on Dr.
    Bonds land
Benjamin Jones lives of John Schutts
    land
Samuel Inloes garden [guardian] for
    Susanna Stone
John Jones lives on Sudden land
Philip Johnson lives on Docter Bond
    land
Anthony Gary
William V. Jenkins
Margait Joyce
Cornel Johns
Magor Jackson lives on the point
William Johnson
Edward Johnson
Elisabeth Jones widdow of Thomas
William Kirk
Thomas Kell
Michal Kimel
Samuel Knox
Nathaniel Knight
Doctor Richard Stone Kingsmore -
    lives on the Joys land
John G.(S?) Kingsmore lives on Jerrut
    Smiths land
Ann Kelso
Francis C. Hallon [Hatton?] lives on
    John B. Howard land
Isaac Kelly lives on Susan Ottry [?]
    land
Elisabeth Key
Ralf Lee
Parker H. Lee

Lomson and Leekes joy(n)ing William
  Yuyn [Young] land
Elizabeth Lynch
Elisabeth Litznigel of Gorge
Elin Litzinger
Gorge Lynch lives on Elizabeth Lynchs
  land
John Laster
Elizabeth Longs
Elexis Lemmon
Moses Liddard
Mariah Linwill
Robert Lusby lives on Joseph Biers
  land
Vallintine Lutes lives on Cristen
  [Christian] Gilback land
Gorge Lash
John Lee
Amos Laney
Thomas Luess [Lewis]
Francis Labard
Abed [Obednego] Langford
Easther Landford [Langford]
Maray Langford
Jethrue Lynch
Partrick Lynch
Joseph A. Latonnandais [In the 1798
  Particular Assessment for
  Middlesex Hundred is an entry for
  Auguste Joseph Lalaouraudais]
Henry Long
Phillip Ladley [Liedley]
Benjamin Hander lives on Wm. Beleys
  [Baily's] land
Valintine Late
Thomas Lukes [Lucas]
Joshua Lynch
Thomas Long lives in Back River Neck
Isaac Lidley [Liedley]
John Mattax living at Levin Stuart
  land
Horn Millers Ares [heirs] joining
  Lidsinger
William Mcferson
William Mcmahen
Loyd McCubins
Joseph Mince
Jacob Madinger
John Martiaig(?)
Thomas Morris
Madcaff Butcher
Cathrin McDermit

Catharine Morris
John McKim juner [junior]
Alexander McKim
John Mycraft
Peter Murray
John Mummy
Cristins Mummy
Isaiah Mankin
Docr. Charls Morse lives at William
  Clarks land
Phenias Murray
John Maizo french man
John McCuller
Luther Mertin [Martin]
Danel Mezter
Charls Manace [Manis?]
John McCubin
William McCubin
John Magness lives on Parker H. Lee
  Land
Mathew McClennon
Jemes McCormack
Doctor Marr [Man?]
Mathew Murray
Thomas Nelson
Harry Nichols
George W. Nichol
Aquilir Night [Aquilla Knight] lives
  at Rigbys Lion tavern
James Nickols lives on Susan Tobeys
  land
John Orem
Sophia Owings
John ODannell [O'Donnell]
Elliott ODonnell
Eliza White ODonnell
Dudley Poor
Benjamin Oyston
William Orem
Elisabeth Orem
Elisabeth Onion
Colombuss Odonnel
Samuel C. Pertick [Patrick]
Israel Peirce
Jemes Perrey lives at Odaniels
  glend[?]
John Perks [Parks]
Pyle and Conway lives on Reids land
William Prise [Price]
William Patterson
John Pornell lives on Mrs. [Mr.?]
  Hartters land

Hannar Porlet [Parlett]
Dobner Partdge [Partridge]
Rose Ann Perty
Susaan Perter [Porter]
Charles Pence Ares [heirs]
Aquiller [Aquilla] Purks
George Presbrey [Presbury]
Marey Presby [Presbury]
Maray Presbury
William Patterson
Charls. Rigley [Ridgley], juner[?]
John Rigley [Ridgley] of Hamton White
  Mash plattason [plantation]
Maray Riley
Edwerd Rollins lives on Jery
  Biddesons land
Isaac Rolins lives on John Hillins
  land
Upton Reid
Isaac Ravin Norwick
Nicholas O Ridgley
William Rollins senr
William Rollins juner [junior] lives
  on his father's land
Isaac Rimmer lives on Cork Shounts
  land
Nicholas Rogers
Jemes Rice
Jesse Rutlige [Rutledge]
John Robarts lives on Mrs. Odonels
  land
George Royston
Thomas Ravin
John Riston
Phillip Rogers sen
William Robarts
Capt Tobias E. Stansbury juner
John Stuart
Elisabeth Sudler
Aquila Starr
Jemes Sudden
Jemes Spilman lives on Hannah
  Barrackmans land
Elisabeth Stansbury widow of George
  Stansbury
Josiah Stansbury
Docter Jacob Small
Henry Statting [Stallings?]¶
William Sarreton (?)
Co. Henry Scuctchts
Robert Stuart
Maray Stommon

Gerrat Samuel Smith
The Airs [heirs] of Isaac Stansbury
John Sumalt
Docter John Simson
Elisha Sollars Airs [heirs]
Thomas Sollars heirs
Docter Jemes Stuart
Richard Shaw
Thomas Shaw
Hany Star
John Strunk
Calip Smiths arrs [heirs]
The ares [heirs] of Samuel Sendle
  [Sendal]
Maray Spear
David Swarts lives at the farm
  formerly Cid Liznik
William Shaw lives on Grove Quarter
Thomas Swetin [Sweeting] lives on
  Mrs. Lynchs land
Samuel Smith
Richardson Stansbury
Darrel (Danel?) Stansbury
Elizabeth Stansbury
William Stevens curled [colored] man
  lives on Penter Boyds land
William Sincler [Sinclair]
John Sincler [Sinclair] lives on
  Benjamin Greens land
Isaac Stallings
Charls Smith
John Sweating
John Stansbury
William Stansbury
John Sudden lives on Mr. Mcmacmakins
  land
Capt. Robert Spence
Job Stansbury
Jems Still lives on Levin Stuart land
Edward Stapleton
Sammuel Strandford(?) [Standiford]
Robert Smith
James(?) Starling
John Stap
William Shaw lives on his fathers
  land
Linch Stuart
Joseph Sterett
John Shaw
Job Smith
Thomas Stuart
Danel Stiver

48

William Stansbury of Wm.
Blancher Sanders
George Stiver
Lues [Lewis] Thomson lives on Josias
  Greens land
Stephen Tredweel [Treadwell] lives on
  John R. Howard land
Richard Talor [Taylor] at R forge
Levy Howard lives on the Young land
  (this entry is lined through)
Robert Turner
Perce Tracey
Thomas Tennent
Henry Thomson
Nathan Turner
William Trimble
Joseph Thomson lives on Joseph Harts
  land
Jemes Thomson lives on Levin Stuarts
  land
Richard Talor
Philimon Towsen
Sarah Trotton
Nathan Tyson
Joshua Tuder
Suseanna Tolly widow of Jems
John Thomas
Benjamin Watz [Watts] living on Mr.
  Hills(?) land
Jemes Wightford [Whiteford] lives on
  Few and Willets land
Samuel Willson living on ... Davis
  land
Elizabeth Wilkenson
John Wilkson lives on Mr. Gibsons
  land
Thomas Wilkeson lives on Justis
  Hoppys land
Abram Williams lives on Mr. Gibsons
  land
John Obrien(?)
Suseanna Wells
John Willet
Francis Vannet
Eve Willcocks
Stephen Wheler
Chattom Waltom
Willet and Dew
Robert Welsh
William Weatherby
Samuel Wilson
Samuel Wilson

Edward Welch
Josiah Watts lives on Jemes Carrols
  land
Robert Welch confiscated propty
Edwerd Woods
Samuel Wortherton [Worthington] Hairs
  [heirs]
John Yeiser
Thomas Wortherton [Worthington]
Juhue(?) Bolding
Peter Boyd
Thomas Barn Doctor
William Rousel
Thomas Branan lives on Crooks land
Jemes Buck
Horriseren(?) Bonett [Bennett]
John Bond lives on Jestus Hoppys land
Levin Baley lives on ... Rigleys land
  formerly Baleys quarter (scratched
  through)
Robert Benson – disputed land with
  the Baleys ...
Nicholis Brian
Asel Barton lives on Thomas Allender
  Ares [heirs] land
Edwerd Brinton lives at Pattersons
  mill
Benjaman Buck Swanson
Muray Bedson [Biddison] widdow of
  Thade(?) lives on Robert Stuert
  land
John Bushep [Bishop] lives on Bucks
  land
Dorcas Buck
Mrs. Sarah Buck
William Bishop
Philip Bemer [Beamer] lives on Gough
  land
Elisabeth Green widow of Joel
Robert Green
The following all owe taxes on 23
  acres of tract called Bushey Neck:
  Cloay Green; Susanah Green; Hammon
  Green; Solomon Green
Gab [Gabriel] Garretson
Muray Green widow of Nathen
William Langton [Langdon]

Accession No. 17664-1, ECP Archivist No. 5

Benja. Osbourn - pt Baddors reserve; pt Robinshoods forrist; pt Drisdales Habitation

Doctr. Edwd. Wakeman - pt Addition; pt Halls Plains; pt Ranshaws Delight; pt Giles & Websters Discovery

Doctr. Josias Meddlemore - The Grove; Palmers forrist; Palmors point; Fannys Inheritance; Websters Enlargment; Meddlemores Defence; Swan harbour; Union; Palmer neglect; Jones Addition; pt of Aarons Spring neck; Edinbourg; pt of Tripple Union; Isington; Meddlemores Angiels

Edwd. Mead - pt Bridewall Dock

Edwd. Sanders - pt Gibsons Ridge

Johns Hopkins - Marino

Robert Clark - Roberts Gardin; pt Good Neighbourhood; Robt & Johns Lot; Roberts Lot; Wheelors Union; Roberton; pt Rachels Delight; Roberts Chance; Little Marlo

Isaac Webster - pt of Friendship; Friendship Addn; Littleworth; Wilsons Range; Rangers Lodge; Websters Contrivence; pt Abbots forrist; Addn to Littleworth; pt Webbs neglect; pt Cristopher Camp; pt of Sidgly; pt of Boston Dever; Websters park; Websters Desire; pt Brooms Bloom

Rowland Kimble - pt of Expectation; Moores Lott; Parkinson; pt Jacksons outlet; Kimble Hazzard; No Name; Kimbles Chance; Kimbles Addn

Thomas Smithson - pt Bills Camp

Jacob Bull - pt Bills Camp; Jacobs Square; pt The Grove

John Norris - pt of Expectation; Norrissis adventure

George Rigdon - Kitter Munster; Rigdons Eskape; Hazzard

Doctr. George Buckanan wido - Murphys Delight; habnab at a venture; Addn to Murphys Delight; goldin forrist; The Land in Skine; Prices folly; Addn to habnab at a Venture; food plenty; Little Kenny;

pt Rogers Choice; one Lot in Baltimore Town

John Willson - pt of Arabia Petre

John Ensor - Darby Hall; Dansels wimsey; pt Cheve Chace; Manner previledge; pt Mount pleasent

Duttin Lane - Beaf Hall; Goodwill; Pork Hall; Hales Adventure; Spring garding; Copper Ridge

Edwd. Fells heirs - Fells Swarthmore; Lancaster; Fells Dale; Darlington; Fells Retirement; Coals Harbour; Two lots in Baltimore town

Samuel Smith - pt East Humphrey

John Edwards - come by Chance

Richard King Stevenson - pt Edwd & Williams; Addition; Goodwill

John Buck, Esqr. - pay my Debts

William Green - pt Mount pleasent; Addn to Mount Pleasent

George Ogg - Morgans Tent; Plumbtree bottom; Hobsons Choice

Saml. Owings - pt Green Spring Punch; Addn; Severn; Comby chance; Mich Meadows; Lewis Fancy; Saplin Hills; timber Levels; Elizabeths Fancy; The Bird Cale; Pleasent Gardin; Roberts Chance; pt Mount Organ

Joseph Merryman - pt Merrymans Lot; Merrymans Addn

Neale Hail - pt the Forrest

John Moal - Jobbs Beginning; Moles quarter; Moles Improvement; Honey point; Ceder Isle; Addn to forbarence; Huckelbery Forrist; Moles purchis

Daniel Stansbury - the prospect; Popler Neck; Strife; The Forceput

Samll. Hooker - Lasting pasture; William; Point lookout; The Addition to william; Hookers Inlargment; the addn; Comby Chance

Edwd. Baxter - pt of Corbins Rest

John Sergent - Adventure; pt of Webbs is Angils

Richard Demmit - pt of Coales Adventure

Major Sabd. Sollers - pt of Kinderton; Timber Neck; Gardiner Addn; Jonas his Chance; Grinworth Resurveyd

John Willmots heirs - Joperdy Tar-
ters; pt Rachels Prospect; pt
Roberts forrist
Capt. Robert Norths heirs - pt Shawan
hunting Ground; pt Hookers chance;
pt Sherideines Grove; pt Chevey
Chace; Addn to sheridnes Grove;
Calf pasture; Browns Chance; Addn
to Greenspring Treverse; pt Gists
Lime pits; pt Adventure; pt Green
Spring Treverse
John Wooden - pt of Parrishes Range
Ann Grant - Grants Addition; Gorsuchs
folly
Thomas Pycroft - pt of Edmonds Camp;
pt of Edmonds Delight
Benja. Meads - Francuses Choice
Baltimore Coty Visiters - pt of
Richard Jons out Let
William Henden - Ishams Garding
James Bosly - Boslys Delight
Anthony Asher - Ashers purchis
John Price Gunpowder - Sefise Town;
Prices hunting Ground
Benja. Bonds heirs - pt of Whitly; pt
Taylors Adventure; pt Robinsons
chance & hog neck
Daniel McComas - pt Grishams College;
Walnut Neck
William Parrish - pt Roberts forrist
Thomas Bond - pt of Harrisons Trust;
Knaves Misfortune; Williams
Delight; Rangers Range; pt of
Bonds forrist; Morgans Lot; pt of
Gibsons rige; pt of Restons Lark
or Chance; Small Quantity; pt of
Osburns Lot; pt of Ables Lot;
Bonds Water Mills
Richard Bond Junr - pt Middle Rige;
pt of Gist Search; Round about; pt
of round about Neighbour
John Cawdrick - Little Britton
Lewis Potee - pt of Thomas Bonds last
Shift; pt of Biz
Staley Durham - pt of Smiths Chance
Isaac Ravin - Albecough; pt of Nor-
wick
Thomas Kelly for Jno. Cawins heirs -
pt of cawins Settlement
William Pike - pt of Whitikers Lot
Thomas Carr - The Regulation

Henry Satyr - Whites Hall; Satyrs
Addition; Egypt; pt Chevy Chace
William Crabtree - pt of Turkey
forrist
Charles Robinson - boslys Pallis;
Robinsons Addn
John Penetent - Jacksons Chance
Mordica Price - Prices Clame; Prices
Outlet; Prices Delight
William Peticote - Peticots Banter;
Newoods Delight
Tobious Stansbury - Stansburys
Chance; Stansburys purchis;
Stansburys puzzel; Stansburys
Neglect; pt of East Humphrys
Daniel Rawlings Junr - Jeopardy; Addn
to Jeopardy
John Bosley - Millers Chance; Billys
Adventure; Boslys meadows; pt of
Hopyard; pt of Gerah; Hookers Addn
William Andrews - Geavers adventure;
addition; Richard Levels; Mulbry
point; pt of Richardsons out let;
Scots Improvement; Adventures
Addn; pt of Ebenezer park; pt of
Jones's Inheritance; Smiths
Discovery; pt of Wintys Test; A
lot in Joppa Shef offis; May More;
Andrews Cave; Foblers outlet; fore
Lots in Joppa
Henry Jones Sadler - pt of Arabia
Petra
William Reaves - Reves Neck
James Elliot - Elliots Resge
John Fuller - Hutchinsons Addn
Abraham Jerrard - Marys Delight;
Hopewell
John Gorsuch - pt of Coles Chance;
Coles Chance & Contrivance; Bought
Dear
Edward Stoxdale - Gosnales Camp;
Stodales Forrist; Stoxdales hils;
Addn to Stoxdales Forrist; Stox-
dales Addn; Edwards Venture; Buck-
ingham privation; pt McClanes hils
Aquilla Massys heirs - Massys Addn pt
Compound; Addn to privilige;
Massys Neglect
William Crabtree Junr - Begin
James Sinclare - Clauens Forrist
Joseph Bosley - pt of Elegas Grove
Reece Bowin - pt of Tipton puzel

Edward Talbot - pt of Thomas Bonds Gift

William Hughs - pt of Triple Union; Hughs Hazzard

Thomas Crabtree - Munster

John Bond son of Peter - Chesnut Rige; pt of Friendship pt of Round about neighbour; Browns prospect

William Goslin - Williams Fancy; Addn to William Defence; The Straight

Richard Rhods - Pearmans purchis

Thomas Denbow - pt of powels choice

John Merryman - Elegys Grove

John Condron - Brown lot

Dennis Garnet Cole - Prices Faviour; Manners Beginnen

Thomas Fowler - Andersons Barnes; pt Sine the Pantea(?)

William Parrish Junr - pt Executer Manegment

Richard Robinson - Tricks & Things; Robinsons Venture; Robinsons Outlet

George Withs heirs - pt Burmans forist

Thomas West - Good Luck

Thomas Dawney - pt of Wornington

Godfery Gash - Skidmers Last

James Preston - pt of Dennists Choics; Prestons Chance; The vinyard; pt Andrews Addn; Dannis's choice improved

Edward Throp - pt of Charles Neighbour

Morris Baker potap - pt of Tanyard

Richard Mitchels heirs - pt of St. Martins Ludgate

William Wheeler - Batchelers neck; Addn to Do; Tiptons Adventure; Hooker Rige

Abraham Taylor - pt of Good Speed; pt of Benjamins Choice; pt of Woods Choice; pt of hobsons Choice

Charles Bailys heirs - pt Moals Success

John Beasey - pt of Selsaid

Peter Bond - Bonds Inheritance; pt of Middlerige; Gists Search; pt Buck park

James Billingsly - Williams lot

Thomas Bond son Peter - pt Lodgsdown Addition; pt of Bedford Resurvyd; Bonds Forrist

Charles Bosley - Batchelors Range; Jacobs Strougle; Batchelors Choice

Robert Chapman - bucks Forrist

Thomas Cole Bush river - pt Bonds Last Shift

Thomas Cole patapsico - Cristophers lot

Richard Cole - pt of Borings Gift

Christopher Cole - planters hils

Thomas Fords heirs - pt of Selsaid

William Harvey - pt of Royall

Mary Scott or Timothy Keen - pt of Stone Ridge

Williams Fells heirs - Coopers harbour; Island Point; Trinkel Field; Gallow Barrow; Carters Delight; Stones Adventure; martins Nest; Little Rome; Five Lots in Baltimore Town

Major Charles Ridgley - Rich Neck; Ridgleys Delight to John Ridgly; Powels Green Spring; Pt of Tanyard; Northamton; The triangle; Ridgleys Whim; pt of Borings Gift; Hails Fellowship; Taylors purchis; Jobbs addn; Ayres desire; Nathaniel hope; pt of adventure; Hampton Court; Ridglys Scrape; Ridglys Fancy; Ridglys Deligence; pt Mathew Forrist; Hannahs lot; Oak hamton; Willkinsons lot; Huntington; pt Edwards's lot; Edwards's Enlargment; Hecters fancy; pt of Parker palis; Timber Neck; chesnut rige

Lawrence Richardson - pt of Avanlas(?) garden

Richard Sampson - Small Value

William Sinclare - pt of Executers Management

Edward Stapilson - Parradice

John Quarterman - pt of Discovery

Capt. Henry Morgan - Knaves Inspection; pt of Taylors discovery; The Chase

Thomas Wrights heirs - Swallow fork; The Island; cadwells outlet; Cuckhold makers hall

Robert Clark - Winters Run - pt Bills Camp

Capt. Perigrine Presbys heirs - pt of Planters Delight; Cullit(?) Point; Black Island; Frisbys Convenicncy

William Stiles - Spring gardin

Thomas Ford Junr - pt Selsaid

William Carter - pt Merrymands Lot

Thomas Wheeler - Wheeler Enlargment; The Beginning; Rough Boughbugh(?); Green Spring; Roses Green; Wheelers Lerch; pt of St. Omers(?); Clarkes park; Mount Pleasent; Long point; The Convencency

Rebecca Potee - pt of prestons Luck

John Garrison - pt of new Park

Capt. William Rogers - Crawlip first Venture; Parkers haven; Kemps Addn; Parrishes Oversight; pt of parrishes Range; Food Plenty; Hogg range; Benjamins Lot; pt of Morgans Delight; Charles's Luck

George Eagers heirs - Jones's chance; Luns Lot; Powels Points

Aaron Rawlings - Willshire

John Bull - pt of Ruffs chance; pt of Howards harbour; Ayres lot; pt French bedford now Wheelers Security; pt of Willsons chance; pt of Austin & Deals chance; pt of Turkey hils

Charles Worthington - pt of Stony Hills; pt of Phillips's Purchis

Thomas Hynes - Hynes' Industry; Hynes's Purchis; pt of hazzard; Hynes's desire; Batchelors Rige

Alexeus Lemmon - Lemmonds Lot

Arther Chinworth - Arthers Lot; Arthers addn

Benjamen Wheeler - pt of Austin & Deals Chance; pt Wheelers Security

David Thomas's heirs - pt of the three Sisters; Isaacs Inlargment

Leonard Wheelers heirs - pt of Wheelers & Clarkes Contrivence; And pearsons Range; pt of Benja. Camp; pt of Brotherly Care

William Few - pt of Thos bounds Gift; harrisons Trust

Isaac Harding - Jones's Chance

Ann Acton - pt of Owings Adventure

John Ford - pt of Gist Search; pt of Reserve; Fords Moinge (Range?)

Edward Tully - Hecters hopyard; Little Meath; Tullys beginning

John Long - pt of Dickinson; Rockey Point; Priviledg

Anthony Enloes heirs - triangle; Enloes Rest; The loe Lands; Duck Neck

Doctr Walker - William Lux heirs - Gills Fancy; Marys plains; Walkers Wilderness; Walker wilderness Continued

Thomas Horner - Carpinters plains; Woods habitation; William chance

John West - pt of Maidens Mount

William Grafton - Graftons lot; Bidmost; pt frenchmans Repose; Brashers Desire; pt of Graftons Gift

Edward Richards - Rattilsnakes rige

Anthony Drew - pt of Drews Enlargment

William Robinson gunpow. - pt of Turkey hils; Archibald's Addition; Better hope

John Giles's Wido - pt of upton

James Gallion - pt of the Agreement; pt of Broome Bloom

Henry Oneal - Murdoughs Chance (entry lined through)

Henry Mores heirs - Good Spead

John Randall - peticots beginning; Rendalls fancy

Roger Randall - pt of Stought

Thomas Johnson Mas. - pt of Bonds lot; pt of Turkey forist; pt Bonds Addn; Nobles Wonder

Samuel Kimble - pt of Expectation

Charles Gilbert - pt of Union; pt of Clarkes Tobacco

John Cawen Junr - pt of Cawins Setttlement

William Mitchel - Cawens Addition

Robert Brierly - Emms Delight; Brierlys Addn; pt of Southampton

Henry Charlton - The Grove

Thomas Stansbury - Stansburys Goodluck; Fathers Cave; Jerico; Lukes goodwill; pt of franklins purchis; Worwick

John Hall Cranbury - pt of cranbury Hall; Do Wido Hall; pt Center

Jacob Young - pt of youngs Delight
Edward Morgin - pt of Simmons Choice
Bennit Neal - Thomas's Beginning;
  Addn. to Do; pt of Maidens bower
  secund
Thomas Hawkins Dear Cre(ek) - pt of
  batchelors Goodluck
Thomas Montgomery - Prices Endever
Benja. Colegate - pt of friends
  Discovery; Colegates last shift;
  Turkey or Timber Range; powels
  point; Ruxton's Range; Benja. Lot
Stephen Onion - pt of Eliza Frenches
  Lot; Bear Island; Onion Fisherry;
  Onions wilderness; Cahoda; Ste-
  phens Fishery; Onions Island;
  Wards Adventure; Margret Delight;
  Littleworth; pt of Ishams Second
  Addn.; Onions Marshy point; Onions
  Gravelly Hills; White Hall; Onions
  Sweatty Banks; pt of hopewell;
  Ishams Addition; pt of Ishams
  Second Addn.; Senica rige;
  Richardsons Reserve; pt of Turkey
  hils; Good Endever; pt of Asbourns
  Lot; Long point; addn. to hope-
  well; Onions Defence; Spanish Oak
  bottom; Onions pasture Ground;
  Addn. to Onions Security Sweaty
  Banks; Selbys hope; Belts Poster-
  ity; Envils Chance; pt of Expecta-
  tion; pt of Thomsons Choice; Heth-
  cots Collage; Rebeccas lott;
  Pabist neck; Addn. to Onion Inher-
  itance; Homer Resurv'd; Onion
  Inheritance Resurvyd.; Cooper
  paradice; Liner Rige; Talbot Cave;
  pt Claxene hope; Cla Hils En-
  larged; Prospect Hills; pt of
  Jerusalem; Little Britton; one lot
  in Baltimore Town; Three lots in
  Joppa; pt Samuells Delight; pt the
  Dock; Onions Second thought
John Lyon - Fathers Bequest
Major Thomas Franklin - Laws Thicket;
  Franklins Delight & Ruths Gardin;
  Hendinham in Buckinham; Industry;
  Ingrams Rich Neck; The Lodge
Robert Adair - pt Margrets Lot; pt of
  Pacas Enlarment & sone (?) rige;
  pt of Arabia Petrea; pt Websters
  Forist

Luke Ravin - The triangle; Lukes
  Adventure; Outlet
Thomas Stansbury - Gorsuch chance;
  Inlow; Selake (?) point; pt of
  Dickinson; Dickinsons Relief;
  Stansburys Adventure; Daniels
  Gift; Stansburys Neadsmust; pt of
  Stansburys Plains; Stansburys
  chance
Samuel Howard - Andersons Lot; the
  Luck
Elizabeth Mathews - Mathews addn;
  Penny Came Quick
Samuel Prichard - pt Moalds Success
James Taylor - pt of Cartor Rest; pt
  jacksons outlet; pt of Good Spead
James Mathews - pt Edwards lot;
  Parsons park; pt of Bonners
  purchis; United Lot
John Clark
  clarkes Meadow; Clarkes town;
  Clarkes Rest
Parker Halls heirs - Stepney; Jerico;
  pt of Sophias Darey; pt of
  Cranbury Hall; comby Chance
George Presbury - Surveyer point;
  Oglesbys Mount; Small Hope; Haps
  hazzard; Groses outlet; Ches Neck;
  Elk Neck
Col. John Hall - Anns Delight;
  Dinnals Swamp; Hall & Bonds
  Discovery; The young Mans Addn
  Compd.; Westmister; Green Spring
  Forrist; Middleboughrough; pt of
  Halls purchis Compd. rent; Bever
  Neck; Hopewell Marsh; Cooks
  Chance; Halls Park; Sheriff Hall;
  Risteaus Security; The ten pound
  purchis; Halls pasture; Halls
  angil; Halls addition; pt Websters
  Inspection; pt Inlargment; pt
  Center
The Reverent Andrew Landrem - Rily
  punch; pt of Punch plantqtion;
  Matsoms Lot; pt of Peters
  addition; pt of Halls purchis
Thomas Brown - pt of Oakington
George Garitson - pt Oakington
Jacob Hanson - pt of Covent gardin;
  Lambes Marsh; pt of abots Forrist
John Bowen Bush river - pt of Bills
  camp; pt of Claxens purchis

Michels Martin - pt of Pole cat neck
William Savory - Savorys Privelege;
Gist Inspecton; Two lots in
Baltimore town; gists addn; Double
trouble; Dandy; Hollonds Lott;
Saverys Farm; Cabbin Neck
Thomas Mitchell - Sisters Downey;
Gilbers adventure
Partrick Lynch - pt of willing; pt of
batchelors Delight; The plains; pt
of Taylors Mount
Thomas Norris - Macedon
Jonathan Starkey - pt of Collingburn
Jonathan Hughs - Williams Fortune; pt
of Roberts Chance; pt of Prestons
Deceit; Hughs's fortune
John Hanson in the neck - pt of the
Narrow Neck; hansons begrug'd Neck
Robert Bishop - pt the Dock; 1/2 Lot
in Joppa
Thomas Baily - Dandy hills
Thomas Mathews - White oak bottam; pt
of mathews Addn; mathews fancy
Williams Jenkins; pt of Mountain; pt
of Arabia petre; pt of Bands hope
Cristopher Shepherd - Knotts Island;
Hogg neck; Shepherds Choice; Shep-
herds Adventure; Shepherds Friend-
ship
John Gray - Taylors Joy
Jane Hughs - pt of hataways hazzard;
pt of Sophias daxey(?)
John Summer - Summer Dear park;
Franklins Choice; pt of Hills Camp
Col. Benja. Pearce - pt of Mount
Serado
Richard Ruff - pt of Strawberry hill;
pt of Cumby Chance; Bonds
Adventure Revis'd; Ruffs Addn.;
Daniels Lot Resurv'd
William Hollis - Jefferys Neck;
Etting; pt of Holliss chance;
Swampy point; Islington; Planters
Neglect; Hollis's hils; South &
North Union
Edward Stevenson - Fellowship; Canaan
Capt. Tobias Stansbury - pt of Mount
Hays; Black Snake point; timber
Swamp; Durham Choice; Rosses
Manner; Stansbury's Inheritance;
Long addn.; Turkey Neck; pt of
Norwich

Robert Hawkins - pt of Margrets Mount
Henry Yoston - pt of Roberts Choice
Solomon Shields heirs - pt of Ferry
Range
William Hamilton - Tuckers Foountain
- Bald hils; Lothain
John Owings - pt of long air
William McClains heirs - Bought wit;
Hesters fancy; pt of Athel
Joseph Miller - pt of Georgs park
William Miller - pt of Georges park
John Stephenson - pt of Edwd. & Wills
Vallys & hils; pt of Molly &
Sallys Delight
Morris Baker - pt of Antioke; pt of
Sammuels hils; pt of Prestons
Deceit
Emanuel Teal - pt of Tanyard; pt of
Robins (?) Camp; Johnsons Range
John Rottingburys heirs - Gallipot
level; pt of pasture Ground;
Jones's Angle
Thomas Sligh - Find me out;
Privilege; Michels beginning;
Johns beginning; pt of Cole hill;
pt of Friendship; Wrights forist;
Tibles's United Inheritance;
Nancys fancy in halls lot; pt of
Comberland; pt of coles Harbour;
Sophias Gardin; pt of Mount ...
(?) Neck; Harrimans Delight;
Richardsons prospect
Thomas Rutter; Salsbury plains
Ann Burk - pt of Stought
Cristopher Randell - pt of George
park; pt of Jopardy; Randels
Meadows; Randels Lot
Luke Trotton - Hopewell; pt of North
Canton; Wall town; pt of Triple
Union; Sure Inheritance
Benja. Bowin - pt of Samuels hope; pt
of Morgans Delight
Abraham Egleston - pt of Witton;
Abbington Enlargment; pt of Comby
chance; pt of Roberts Choice
Thomas Demmit - Upper Spring Neck;
Jones Neglect
Zachariah Gray - Nashes Rest; pt of
Witton; Maidens Out; Grays
Convenency
Robert Wilkinson - Landisell; Wilkin-
sons chance; Wilkinsons Spring

George Chancy - pt of Hollisis Refuse
Richard Hendon - pt of Chevy Gardin;
pt of Avarilas gardin
John Hurd - Roles Chance; Minton
Job Evins - pt of Fox Hall; Evinsis
Meadows; Addn. to Evins's Meadows;
Dorseys Milfrog
Archibald Rollos heirs - Rollos
Adventure
John Thrift - Thomas's Neglect; Addn.
to Thomas's neglect
Alexander McComas Junr - horse Range
Thomas Presbury - Oxford
John Suynard - Bonds Discovery; pt of
Colegates forist; Chesnut rige;
Howards Chance; St. Albans;
Swynards Delight; pt of Prestons
luck
Benja. Norris - pt of E (* in later
debts books a tract named Everly
Hills is listed) Hills; pt of
Bixe; Shepperds range; Gibsons
Rige; Addition to Gibsons Rige
William Debritter - pt of Sallys
Delight & Good providence
William Woods heirs - pt of Arthers
Choice
Thomas Green - pt of dear bit; pt of
Dear bit & pt of Salisbury
William Lewis - pt of Howards Fancy;
The Friendship
Charles Motherby - pt of Mt. organ;
Motherbys Adventure
Susana Butler - the Hope
Henry Stevenson - Addn. to Fellow-
ship; The Daisy
John Mathews - Majars Choice; Mathews
Enlargment; Shipping Dock
William McComus heirs - pt of
Grissums Colege; pt of Littleton
John Timmons - pt of Friendship
Thomas Norris potao [patapsco] - pt
of Early hills
Errick Errickson heirs - Erricksons
Garison
George Harryman - pt of Comberland;
project; Harrymands Outlet;
Harrymans hope; pt of Shaws Fancy;
pt of Shaws Delight; pt of Shaws
privelege
Thomas Litton - pt of Margrets Mount;
Littons fancy; pt of Arabia Petrea

Charles Baker - pt of Porke forist;
The Oblong
John Nelson - pt of Birr
Benjamin Webbs - Lingan; Markland
Friendship; Timber Neck; Pleasent
Spring & Ary hills
Capt. William Dulliam (Dallam) -
Spries Inheritance; Eliza Chance;
pt of Dullams Self preservation;
Three Brothers; pt of Jerusalem;
pt of Morefields
Solomon Kellers heirs - pt of
hazzard; pt of Refuge; Shomakers
hall; Paridic; Disapointment
John Harriman - Richardsons forist
Abraham Ravin - Fellowship; Cox's
fancy; pt of Richardsons Neglect;
Lukes addn.; Phillamans lot;
haphazard; Gay Silvina; Wheelers
Beginning; Gay Good fellowship
Thomas Hutchins - pt of Hutchins
Neglect; Hutchins lot
Alexander Young - pt of Southhampton
George Farmer - pt of new westwood;
pt of Margrets Mount
Thomas Shea - pt of out Quarter; pt
of new west wood; Murdocks Chance
James Prichard - pt of Hughs Enlarg-
ment; pt of Hughes choice
Samuel Wallace - Cobbs Delight; pt
of Arabia Petrea
John Gill - pt of Batsons forist;
Gills Range; pt of parish range;
Millers Gain; Gills Prospect
Solomon Rowles - pt of Jones Adven-
ture; William the Conquerer;
Jacobs delight
Isaac Hitchcock - Bednalls Green
Joshua Sewell - Arabia Felex
Thos. or Nathal. Brothers -
Steponsons plains
Oliver Harriots heirs - hunting
Quarter
Thomas Miles - pt of Caprice
Roger Donohues heirs - pt of
Southampton; Donohuse Strife
Penelope Die - pt of Gerat; Taylor
hall; Thos. & John Co'keys
Meadows; Logdown; wasons Farm
Widow Darby - pt of todds Range; pt
of darby

Daniel Durbin - pt of Durbins Chance; pt of Tripple Union

Richard Johns - The Rich bottom Corrected

Ulick Burk - coxes forist

John Cooper - Elishas lot; Coopers Range; The Desarts of Arabia; Coopers Addn.; Cullins park

Capt. John Stinchcomb - Stinchcombs Reserve; Hecters Chance; pt of pistole; Addn. to Pistole; Stinchcombs hills

Isaac Wood - Chesnut rige; Isaacs Lot; Woods Meadows; Wilborns Venture

William Towson - Vulcania; pt of Gunners range

John Cooks heirs - pt of Maidins Mount; pt of paradice

Thomas Gilbert - the Division

Thomas Arnold - pt of Whitcers Rige

Benja. Ingram - Michaels Addn.; Michaels Chance

Jacob Giles - Johnsons Delight; Bourn; pt of Elberton; Simsons Second hay yard; Giles's Addn.; pt of James's park; The land of promise; The Stop; Brotherly love; pt of Johnsons Rest; pt of Friend Ship; pt of Arabia Petrea; pt of Eightrup; half Webs Neglect

James Wells - Wells Care

Joseph Ranshaw - pt of Clarkes Dunmuryinantown

Col. Thomas White - pt of Sophias Darey; The Dary Enlarged; Simmons Neglect; Halls Plains; The Royall Exchange; pt of hazzard; pt of Gravely hils; Eaton; pt of Mount serado; pt of Abbots Forrist; Jonas's Addition; pt of Eightrup; ha ha indeed; The woodyard; Trancilvania; Hammonds hope; Manreal; Halls Rich Neck; pt of Turky hill; Hathaway hazzard; Swansbury; Rumny Royall; Delph Island; pt of Constant Friendship; the out let; Constantinople; Antrum; Laudemon; Little hopewell; pt of littleton; Harrison Resolution; Kilkenny; Londonderry; Paradice; Hickery Rige; pt of United Friendship

Hathaways Trust; Gays Enlargment; pt of Neighbour affinity; Pacas Second Addn. to Water Mils; Leigh of Leighton; Keytone (?) Range Resurvy'd in ha ha indeed

Michael Gilberd - Halls pipe; pt of Gibsons Chance; pt of the Union; pt of Clarks Tobeco (Tobacco)

Richard Gott - Gotts hope; Addn to Gots hope

Shelton Standifer - the worlds End

Jnathan Hanson - Mount Royall; Hansons Chance; pt of Edwards lot; The Dusty Miller

Nichs. Hutchins - Hutchens Neglect; Hutchens Lott

Winston Smiths heirs - Gaths Neglect; Martins Rest; pt of planters Delight; Timber proof; pt of Walltown Addn; Goldsmiths Hall; Mathews Neglect

John Poteet - Bear Range; Good Luck

Alexander McKenly - Michl. Hazzard

Thomas Tipton Junr - Williams begining

John Everit - Cockins Lott

Ford Barnes heirs - Dooleys Begining; Barnes Neglect; pt of Repulta; Barnes Delight

Joseph Willson - pt of Daughters Chance; Willsons chance; pt of neighbourhood

James Death - Daughters Chance; the Creek plantation; pt of Neighbourhood

William Greenfield - pt of Greenfield Double purchis

Peter Goslin - Goslins Camp; Absolams place; Addn to Goslins Camp; Goslins purchis

William Standifer; pt of hutchins Addn.

Henry Thomas - pt of Rachels Delight; The addition; Henrys pleasure; Henrys Hope

Nehemiah Hicks - Timber hall; Halls forist

John Standifers heirs - Franklin begining and Nancys Ending

John Boreing - Borings gift; Borings forrist; Borelings Meadows

Cornelious Howard - pt of Cornelious & Margrets lot; Joshuas gift; Howards Square; Security; Hurds Camp; Calf pasture; Howards Enheritange; pt of Ashmans Delight; Water oak Rige; Howards Contrivance

Peter Bingan - Bingans Venture; Peters Discovery

Thomas Woodards heirs - Shomakers hall; Hoggnorton

Aquila Carr - pt of prices Goodwill

John Stoxdale - Brotherly love

Joshua Hardisty - pt of Clauins purchis; Timber Swamp; pt of powels Choice

Joseph Perigo - pt of Cradon on the hils

David Carlisle - Carlisle park

Nattl. Davis - Little Mountain; Davids hope

Thomas Broad - Bussels

Samll. Smith gunpowder - Fools Refuse; Mathews Dum purchis

Mark Guishard - Griers Discovery; pt of Avarilas Gardin

William Banks - Banks Delight

Joshua Owings - owings Choice; Shiloh Cumpleted; The addition to Shiloh Compd.

Benja. Knight - Planters Rige

Thomas Johnson Fork - pt of Jemaca; Jacobs Lott; pt of Hutchins Addn.

Heathcot Puket - Jacobs Inheritance; Good hope

Ann Moulton - ptof Woods Close

Thomas Wells Junr - Rogues Range; Thomass Adventure; Wills Meadow; The hollow neck; Jacobs Well; Wellsis prospect; Addition to Wellsis prospect

James Gardiner - Hawkinsis Desire

Thomas Gorsuch - pt of Friend Ship

John Green - Green pallis; Green Lot

William Lynches heirs - pt of Liduan; pt of Jonas's Inlargment; pt of heirs Green; pt of poplar Rige; Hopes Island; Industry; Bagsfords Fortune; Watkins Neck; Prevelege; Batchelors Delight; Tharrvles (Harrils?) Neck

William Wrights heirs - pt of Sign the painter

Charles Green - pleasent Gardin

Robert Green - pt of Burmans Forrist

Michll. Gladman - Harklepool

John Morgan - pt of Burmans forrist

Edwd. Perrigo's heirs - pt of Burman forist

Benja. Legoe Junr - pt of Warington; Legoes Chance; legoes Troughble (Trouble); Halls rige

Joseph Taylor - Continuence; Addn to Taylors Range; Addn To Shomakers Hall; Friends pt of Darby Hall; pt of the Forist

William Hill - Divers Chance; Worington

Nathll. Ayres - Buck Range

Hugh Sollars - the hope; Cuckhold makers Hall

Lewis Igoe - friends Discovery

Robert Scott - Coal Hill; pt of Morefields

Garvis Gilbert - pt of Mathews Neglect

William Talbots heirs - pt of Ogg King of Bashan; parsons Outlet Witheall Addn

Laben Ogg - Hicks Adventure; pt of Bonds forist

John Atkinson - broad Neck & Clements Den; parkers Folly; Dogwood Rige; Landito; Parkers Choice; Marsh

Alexander Lawson - Borings Range; pt of Ferry Range; Buckners Improvement; Swan harbour; borings pasture; Bred & Chese Mill; haphazzard; happi be luckey; pt of Daniels wimsey; Buckners purchis; Bails Discovery; addn. to pore Jemimy Mans (Jamaicamans) plague; The Groves; Fords Fancy; pt of addn. to pore Jemimy Mans plague

Samuel Harryman - Sedgwell; Sampsons faviour; Smiths Addition

Luke Griffin - pt of Leaf Jurnifer; pt of Refuge; Phillips Swamp; Williams hope; pt of Abbots forist; Hopes Addn.

Capt Richard Dullam - pt of Arabia Petra; Miles Improvement; pt of Neighbourhood

Nathll. Stenchoms heirs - Batchelors hope; Batchelors addition; pt of pistole; Addition to pistole

Walter Ashmore - pt of Arabia petre

Ephram Gover - pt of Elberton

George Batts - pt of Wests faviour; pt of Knights increse

William Johnson - Farvers Favour

James Crawford - Crawfords double purchis

John Colegate - pt of John & Thomas Forrist

Oliver Cromwell - pt of Maidins Choice; pt of Cromwells Chance resurvd.

George Rock - pt of Elberton; Contrivance

Joseph Cromwell - Dear park; Cromwells Enlargment

James Carrol - pt of harrises trust

John Dunn - pt of Arabia petrea

John Dawney - Yorks hope

Michll. Eastwood - pt of Margrits purchis

Thomas Farmer - pt of Eliza Frienches lot

William Fitch - pt of Smiths Chance

William Burton - pt of Whiteacres Rige; pt of the agreement

Solomon Gallion - pt of the Agreement

James Griffith - Cristmas Eve; Griffiths Mount

Thomas Gibbons - Blunder

John Gregory - pt of privelidg

John Hawkins - The Mistake; French Mans neglect

Miss Mary Hanson - Hansons Wood lot; Marys Meadow

John Robert Camwell- Small value

Joseph Jones - pt of Arabia

Richard Sedwith - Johns Begining

James Lee - pt of Simmons Choice; pt of Planters paridice; Duldps Mistake; pt of Isaacs Inheritance; Isaacs Doublepurchis; pt of Mountain

Thomas Porter - Norton hall

John Parrish Junr - pt of parrish forist

Thomas Phelps - pt of Jones's Inheritance; pt of Arabia petre

Edward Parrish - pt of parrishes forist; pt of clarkes park

Beaver Spain - Turks range Nobles desire and pearsons privelidge

Stephen Owings - Batchelors hall

Thomas Richardson - Timber hils

Col. Nathan Rigby heirs - Philips purchis; Browns Discovery; pt of Parkers chance; pt Rigbies hope

Nicholas Smith - Welches fancy

Capt. John Risteau - Credentia; Risteaus Enlargment; St. George's plain; Benja. prospect

John Roberts Joppa - Goldsmiths Neck; Arthurs Delay; pt of Woolf harbour; Two lots in Joppa

John Stokes - pt of planters Delight; pt of Goldsmiths Hall; pt of Timber proof; pt of Walltown habitation; pt of Mathews Neglect

Francis Bondfield - pt of Arabia Petre

John Stansbury - Carrs lot Resurvy'd

John Tipton - Batchelors begining; Benja. Addition

Richard Wells - pt of Arabia petre

Doc. William Lyon - pt of Gists lime pits; three lots in Baltimore Town; Lyons Den; Spring Gardin; Madcalfs Addition; Murrys meadow; pt of Rich levels

Capt. John White - Whites level; Small addition; Mill lot

Jacob Cord - Cooks Rest

William Perkins - pt of Eightrup; pt of Dae

Solomon Wheeler - Hooker property

James Garrison - Newpark

Robert Dutton - Merrikins inheritance for Ever

Andrew Magill - Stephens hope; Belfast; Magills Choice Resurv'd

William Coine - pt of hunting Quarter

Henry Addams - pt of Cullinsons Choice; pt of previlige

William Cole Dear Creek - pt of Arabia Petre

Moses Paris - pt of Arabia petre

William Nickolson hrs - Nicholsons Manner

John Price Garrison - Tommy's Choice

Edward Ward - pt of Arabia petre

Jonathan White - prospect
Pollard Keane - pt of good Neighbour-
hood
Francis Jenkins - Frankford
Alexander Hill - pt of Arabia petre
John Penn - Hopes lot
Walter Billingsly - pt of Bonds lot;
Bonds Addn.; pt of Porke Forrist;
Loves Addn.; Warford; Billingslys
lot; pt of Bonds fortune
James Kelly - pt of Gist Serch; pt of
Friendship; Kellys Delight
Daniel Preston - Daniels lot;
Prestons Choice
John Hammond Dorsey - pt of Wignols
Rest; Webit; pt of Watertons
neglect; Foxhall; pt of owners
landing
Abraham Wright - Isaac Wrights Range
Thomas Stoxdale - Stoxdales Abode
William Willson Pipe Cr. - Longvally
The Revt. Benja. Bourdillions heirs -
pt of Bonds plesent hils; 5 lots
in Baltimore Town
Thomas Durbin; pt of Prestons Deceit;
pt of Chance
Capt. Nicholas Gay - Gays Woodyard;
Annapolis; Spring Neck; Maxwells
hope; Solders Delight; pt of Coles
harbour
Abraham Green - pt of Goose harbour
Francis Rider - the wedg
John Chalk - pt of ogg King of Ba-
shan; parsons outlet & wetherall
Addn.; pt of Ogg King of Bashan
Thomas Gittings - Clerke Forrist; pt
of Thomsons Choice; Hutchins
begining
Saml1. Underwood - pt of Friend Ship
Saml1. Forts heirs - pt Friend Ship;
Addn. to Do
William McQueen - Crambury plains
Thomas Bradly - pt of Arabia petrea
Adam Kendrickson - Dukes pallis
Jacob Rowles - pt of tripple union;
Sampsons addition; Harrystone; pt
of Johnson; Ardingtoons adventure
Sarah Bond - pt of Harrisons Forist;
pt of abots Lot
Absolum Brown - pt of hunting worth;
pt of Jameses Addition

Reverent Hugh Deans - Staxdil More;
pt of William the conquer
Saml1. Howell - Bilings Gate; Levels
addition; Buskfield Venture; Lof-
lands Neglect & howels contri-
vance; Johnsons bed; Johnsons
Rest; Knavery prevented; pt
Martins Ludgate; Howels Dream
Capt. Phillip Jones - pt of Johnson;
Thomas Addn.; Westmister; pt of
pasture ground; pt of Tripple-
union; Dickinson; pt of Darbey;
1/3 of Sewalls Relief; pt addn. to
McClanes hills
Thomas Coleate - pt of John &
Thomas's forist
Peter Carroll - pt of Expectation; pt
of Bartons Chance
Roger Newmans heirs - Jones's Range;
Newmans Delight
Col. Willm. Young - pt of Sewalls
fancy; pt of ...(?); A lot in
Joppa; a lot in Baltimore town;
Narrow Bottom; Dividend; Little
Worth
Saml1. Webb - St. Anns Lot; Spittle
Croff; pt of B...(?) hope; pt of
Belch abode; Rough stone "this is
by paten(t)"; pt of Brothers Dis-
covery; Ranchaws last purchis; pt
of Giles & Websters Discovery
Richard Clark - Clay; pt of Clarks
park
Nathan Smith - Contrivance; Newsons
Meadow
Hugh Morgan - pt of Brothers Discov-
ery
William Daugherty - Thomas & Mary's
repose - Roberts Choice
John Loney - Porters half & the
Enlargment
Walter James heirs - Blackwolf Neck;
Fells range
Robert Sanders - pt of James's
forrist
Saml1. Youngs heirs - Young's Escape
Francis Rusels heirs - Danielston;
Waberton
William Logsdown - Conners Delight
Thomas Cook - Cook'es purchis
Luke Mercer - Mercers Chance; Rawlys
Neck

Capt. James Phillips - Begining
Choice; pt of hining Worth; Mates
angils; Chelsy; Lamberth marsh;
James Park; pt of Covent Gardin;
pt of James addn.; Browns Chance;
James's Addition; Fraternity; Leaf
Junifer; Crabb Hills; Collins
Meadows; Un(d)er Eating; Chilbury
Neck

Edward Oyslet - Long look for

Richard Parrish - Bachelors fancy; pt
of Clarkes park

Joseph Arnold - pleasent level;
Arnold's Arbour

Stephen Willkinson - Northamton

Wason Wheeler - Wheelers lot

Aquilla Gilbert - pt of the Agreement

John Hall son of Aquila - pt of
Aquilas Inheritance; Harmans
wantown or Goldsmiths Enlargment;
Goldsmiths Rest; Perserve; pt
Minors Adventure

Capt. Willm. Bradford - pt of the
Enlargment; Bradford Barrens; pt
of Comby Chance; pt of Osburn
Addition

Ignatious Wheelers - pt of Wheelers &
Clarks Contrivence; Andpearsons
Range; Benjamins Camp; pt of
brothers Care; Wheelers & Clarks
Contrivence

James Scott - pt of Benjamins Camp;
James's forrist; Addn. to James's
forist; Scotts Close

Alexander Thomson - pf ot Willsons
Choice

Francis Watkins - pt of Bosleys
Expectation; pt of Arthors Choice

Richard Jacks - Jacks Delight; The
fountain of Friendship

Benjamin Jones - hansons choice

Joseph Hopkins - pt of Phillips
purchis

Humphry Wells Stokes heirs - pt of
Westwood; Hermon town Resurv'd;
Ebenezers Lot

John Carvil - Pools Island - Compound
rent

Henry Wetherall - Lowes Neck; pt of
Samuells hils; pt of Johns
Interest; Lewis's purchis; Lining
Manufactory; Hansons Neglect; pt
of Mathews Double purchis

William Bonds heirs - Addition;
Buckrange; Lawsonses Pasture;
Harriots Delight alias Fancy

Thomas Harris widow - pt of Mount
hays; pt of previlege

Robert Patison - pt of Wicteurs
(Whitakers) Rige; Miles End; pt of
Addn.

Joseph Johnson - pt of Mountain

Sarah Boreing - Hails Folly; Two lots
in Baltimore Town

Principio Company - Winters Run; Long
point; Rogers Road; maidens out;
pt of Upton Court; pt of Jonas's
Inheritance; The plains Resurv'd;
the welch Knavery prevented;
Grindon; Willmots Folly; Sheridines Discovery; Twidiston;
Companys Lotts; Willmots Refuse;
Willmots neglect; pt of Kingsbury

Thomas Downawin - pt of the Narrow
Neck

Walter Dallas - Hopewell; Bushey
Neck; The outlet to bushey Neck;
Kindness Resurv'd; Tryden;
Littleworth

Samll. Stansbury - Long Island; The
Addition; Venture Not

Jabaz Murry - Merrymans Grotto; Addn.
to Merrymans Grotto

Richard Rutter - Timber rige; Valient
Hazzard

Josephus Murry - Elegys farm; Murrys
farm; addn. to Joshuas lot

George Cole - Stone Range

Barzeleel Forstures heirs - pt of
windlys Rest

John Camrons heirs - Hoggpoint

Samll. Syndall - pt of Dearbit

Jacob Lusby; pt of Chilbury Hall; pt
of Do. Resurv'd; pt of hathaways
Trust; pt The out Let

Richard Keen Prince Georges Coty -
heirs - pt Clagetspoint

William Beaver - pt of Marys Delight;
pt of Neighbourhood; pt of Aribia
Petre

Thomas Archer - pt of Unkils Goodwill

Mabury Helms - pt of Parrishes fear

William Wells - pt of Bonds pleasent hils

William Davis - pt of Antioke

Cristophur Dukes - Hab nab at a venture; pt of Norwick

William Murphy - Scotsmans Desire; The wite Oakbottom; Dorseys Addn.; Robaracum

Skepwith Cole - pt of Stone Hill; pt of Arabia petre; pt Batchelors Goodluck; Henlys Enlargment

John Pribble - Neighbours Good will; pt of Wests faviour

William Parlet - Parlets Addn; Parlets fancy

John Jones - Rutledge Delight

John Brierlys wido - pt of Arabia petre

Edward Flanagin - pt of Out Quarter; Calebs Necesaty

Capt. John Peca - pt of Gibsons park; pt of Warter Mil; pt of addn to water mil; Pecas Enlargment & Stone Rige; Security; pt of Chilbury Hall; Pecas Chance; pt of maidins bower Secur'd; pt of comby Chance; pt of Pacas park; Pecas meadows; Askins Hope; Prices Delight; Belgrade; Trancilvania

John Bond; pt of James Park; pt of Prospect; Bons Tanyard; Two lots in Joppa

John Clark potapsco; Hopewell; Clarks lot

Robert Cross - pt of Cargoforguis

Timothy Murphy - Murphys hazzard

William Webb - Webbs discovery

William Bearman - Williams lot; Williams Defence; the addition to Wm. Defence

James Brice - Brices purchis Corrected

Richard Owings - pt of Sevets levels

Daniel Barrel - pt of Broads Improvement; Two Lots in Baltimore town

James Wells Junr - Hickory Bottom; James's fancy

Walter Tully - Traces level; Taylors Mount Dixons Chance and long point; Pimlico; Nothing Worth; Hall hils; Littons improvement;

Speedwell; Lovepoint; Tolleys hill; Tollys Double purchis; Tollys purchis; pt of Richardsons outlet; Bettys Choice; United Friendship

Jeames Kean - pt of out Quarter; Little Scotland

Michll. Hodskins - Hodskins chance

Jonathan West - pt of maidins Mount

Gabriel McKensey - Gabriels Choice

Talbot Risteau - carters Rest; Richards hope; Hebron; Two lots in Joppa

James Whiteers (Whitaker) - Stoney Batter

Thomas Casebolt - pleasent Vally

Thomas Frazier - Johnkins Delight

Cristopher Sewall - Sewalls Defence; Saplin Rige

Robert Gilcrest - Cathermaath; Mountpleasent; Rapho

Charles Kelly - Weedings Choice; Mallow

Charles Kezzey (?) - Youngs Chance

John Welch - Perseverence

Thomas Levens - Thomas's Choice

Charles Bolton - pt of Bonds Gift

James Rigbee - pt of Batchelors Goodluck; pt of brothers Discovery; pt of paradice

William Odells heirs - Arnolds Chance; Odles Addition; Adels Expectation

Thomas Harrison - Two lots in Baltimore town; pt of Roberts park; pt of Ashmans hope; Markantile Strugle; Harrison Dock; pt of James's park; pt of Ownen Landing; Griffiths Adventure; pt of Nangemy; Lines Tents; Limce Addn.; Addn. to Harrimans Meadows; Cowins Neighbour; the Cord Wood; Murrys plains Resurv'd; Harrisons Improvement

Samll. Gilbert - John & Isaac's Lot

William Arnold - pt of Hammonds hope

Nattl. Rigbe Junr - pt of parkeses chance; pt of Rigbies hope

John Holland - pt of Bonds forist

Moses Ruth - pt of Umleys Goodwill

Moses Ruters heirs - pt of Adventure

Guy Little - Agury; Hunting Neck

Christian Piggslar - pt of Great
Meadows
John Hartshorn - pt of Arabia Petre;
Rosemary Rige
William Elliot - pt of Giles & Web-
sters Discovery
Cooper Oram - pt of Maidens Choice
Joseph Green - pt of Bowens purchis
Capt. Darby Lux's heirs - Two lots in
Baltimore town; Moslinton; pt of
Grooms Chance; Darby Shire; Luxes
Contrivance; pt of Coles Chance;
pt of Edwards Enlargment
Saml1. Bowen - pt of Bowers prospect;
pt of Jones's Range; Jones's addi-
tion; pt of Jones's range & Ryders
Industry
Edward Bowen - Cossils Hills
Dickson Stansbury - Dublin
Joseph Chew - pt. of Bachelors good-
luck
Thomas Durbin - Hughs Choice
Henry Beach - pt of Maidens Bower
Securd.; Millers Delight
James Bowens heirs - pt of bowens
purchase; Little Goos harbour
Nicholas Rogers - pt of Rogers's
Choice; Nathans forist; Two lots
in Baltimore town
Zachariah McCubbin - pt of Ashmans
hope; Turkey thicket; pt of part-
ner Ship
James Welch - Trawmord; Angles
fortune
Volentine Carback - Molys Garden
Edward Sprigg - Gassaway Rige
Isaac Litton - pt of Arabia Petre; pt
of neighbour hood
Robert Baniker - pt of Stout; timber
p'int
Thomas Waltham - pt of Conclusion
Daniel Deaver - pt of Turkey hils &
Strawbery hils
Loyd Goodwin - Howards Invertation;
Lots in Balt. town
John Woody - pt of Neighbourhood; pt
of Arabia Petra
William Willson Solders Delight -
Willsons Adventure
George Hails - Hails Fellowship;
Teagues park
John Whyat - pt of Knighs Increce

Thomas Bond Junr - tower hill; Miles
Improvement; pt of Caprice
Joseph Bardel - Peters Second
adventure; Molenes Resolution
Saml1. Shiply - Greenbury Grove
Mich11. McQuire - patience Care
Robert West - Long Acre
Doctr. David Ross - pt of Sewells
Relict (Relief)
Saml1. Durbin - pt of Edmuns Camp;
Bilbury Hall; Durtrams first addn
to Bilbury Hall; Do Second Addi-
tion to do; Do third Do; pt of
Edwins Contrivence; Friends Advice
Charles Gorsuch - Canaan
Alexander McComus son John - pt of
Strawbury hils; Deavers Addn
Henry Monday - pt of Howards Forest
William Watson - pt of Mathews forist
Stephen Gill - pt of Batsons forist
John Baxter - pt of Batsons forist;
Baxters folly; Addn to Baxters
Choice
Thomas Hudson - pt of Batsons forist
Joseph Lee - pt of Arabia petre
Jacob Combest - George Hall; Smiths
Folly
Eliza Scott - Scotts Improvement; pt
of Bier
Daniel Scotts heirs - pt of Meritons
lot
George Hays - pt of halls plains;
Prichards Security
Aquila Scott - pt of Bills Camp;
Scots Hopewell; Scots Range;
Addition to Trust; Trust
William York - pt of Sallys delight &
Good Providence
Benja. Culver- Browne Entrence
Ralph Pile - Isaacs Delight
Thomas Gist - pt of the Adventure;
Lime pits; Friend Ship
John Starkey - Greers Park; Greers
Improvement
John Pendal - pt of friendship; pt of
Gist Serch
Joseph Sollers - pt of Corbins Test;
pt of Jons's Range & Industry
John Robinson plantor - Treaton
John Holt - Comby Chance
John More - Comberland
John Copeland - pt of friendship

Bush River Company - Caudi (Creeds?)
Begining; Miles's forist; pt of
friend Ship; Brokins Island; pt of
Noviscotia; pt of Wheelers Enlarg-
ment; pt of comby Chance
Notingham Company - pt of Richardsons
Outlet; Boughtons forist; Jacobs
Choice; Further addn. to Bough-
tones forist; Addn. to Do; Back
Lingan; The three sisters; Bettes
Inheritance; mathews Choice; New
Years purchis; pt of Sewalls
fancy; Hutchins Begining; simons
Choice; pt of Richardsons neglect;
pt of Wignols Rest; Notingham
Moses Merryman - pt of Merrymans
Delight
Doct. Holidays heirs - 3 lots in
Baltimore Town; Goshan Resurv'd
John Hamton - pt of Contest; pt of
Halls park
William Arnold potapsco - Hammonds
richland
John Frazer - pt of Forrist;
Elizabeths Delight; Deep point
James Rowland - Bear hils
Benja. Whips - Wips purchis
Samuel Smith Swan Cre(ek) - Margrets
Mount
William Rigdon - Friend Ship
Thomas Renshaw - Clarks Denmoney in
Antrim; pt of Giles & Websters
Discovery; Renshaws Desire
Abraham Renshaw - pt of Giles &
Websters Discovery
William Pearce - Mollys Industry
John McClain - The folly; Addn. to
McClains hils
Jonathan Plowman - plowmans park;
Bucks Thicket
John Plowman - Plowmans fancy;
plowmans Adventure
Thomas Bently - Hill Spring
William Cross - Crosses Meadow
William Kelly - pt of Green spring
Traverce; pt of Green Spring punch
Henry Perigo Junr - Henrys Lot
Benja. Rickets - pt of Conclusion,
Compound
William Gist - Woolf Den; Gist
Enlarged; The Addn.
John Robinson - Robinsons begining

Greenbury Dorsey - pt of Nangemy; pt
of the three Sisters
William Shaw - pt of Todds Range
William Tipton - pt of Tiptons puzzle
William Barney - pt of Morgans
Delight; Barneys Inheritance
William Hawkin's widow - pt of
Parrishes Range
Amon Butler - Halls Approach
John Jinkins - pt of Mount Organ &
Jinkins Addn.; Jinkins Repose
John Paca Junr - pt of Gibsons Park;
Delph; Delph neglect; pt of Addn
to Watermil; Goldsmiths hall; pt
of Pacas Park; pacas Convenancy;
pt of Chilbury Hall; pt of
WaterMils; pt of Pacas Delight
Amos Garret - Hazzard Enlarged;
mathews Chance; Watkins Inlet; pt
of Cooks Denpurchis; Jacksons
hazzard
Nathan Richardson - Colrain
William Smith potap. - Harrimans
pasture
Capt. William Bond - Female Care; pt
of Midsummers hils; Ferbury Neck
Richard Son Stansbury - pt of addn.
to James pore mans plague; pt of
Balliston
Edward Norris - pt of prospect; The
End
Phillip Gover - pt of Repultra
Richard Pinkham - pt of Mathews
forist
George Baily - Bailys Lot
Thomas Cockey - Turkey Cock Ally
Saml1. Busey - Kellys Delight
William Cawen - pt of Tripple Union
Alexander Baker - Crishans Lot; pt og
Brothers Expectation
Roger Bishop - Batchelors Begining
John Thomas - Thomas's choice
Willm. John & Rubin Boring - Three
Brothers
Phillip Addleman - Phillips Bough
John Keyes - Keys Industry
John Whips - Turkey Range
Samuel Whips - Mollys habitation
James Walters - Kingsail
William Winchester - Collinton;
Winchester lot; Little Britton

James Richards - Jones's farm; North
Carolina; 3 lots in Baltimore
Town; Batchelors Choice; Carolina
Felex; Spring gardin; pt Humphry;
Drunkards halls; pt of Spicers
Inheritance

Nicholas Peticoat - Peticoats hope

Thoms. Biddison - Harbour; Addition
to Harbour

Samuel Tipton - painters Level

Lancaster Iron Works - Harnmans
Landing; Carrols Scrutiny; Carrols
pursuit; pt of folks forist;
Batchelors Neighbour; Buck lodge;
Carrols Search; Fannys Neighbour;
Slight Discovery; pt of buck
Range; Jeames's park; Oblong &
Inloes Choice; Roboraries; Pistole
& Addition; Borings Landing;
Buckscrape; Dundee; Greenbury
Swamp; What you please; Harrimans
Range; Carrols pursuit

Jervis Biddeson - Sisters hope;
Goosberry Neck

Joseph Morgan - pt of Maidens Mount;
pt of Brothers Discovery; pt of
Paradice; Faviour; Dear bought &
nothing Got; Morgans Addn.

Stephen Price - Long looked for; Long
track; James Meadows

John Cook - Welches Adventure (lined
through)

Ambros Geogham - Ambros's Lot

Joseph Rogers - pt of Arabia petre

William Seabrooks - Taylors farm;
London

Joseph Presbury - pt of Collects
Neglect

Thomas Davises heirs - Dukes Disovery
Corrected

William Bennet - pt of Arabia petre;
pt of Websters Inspection; pt
Inlargment; pt of Center

Peter Laman - pt of Great Meadow

William Gorsuch - mathews Farm;
Mathews Meadow; pt of Mathews
Addn.

Edward Lee - Gardiners Farm

Abell Brown - Owens Outland plains;
Hunters Chance; Fine Soil forist

Absolum Barney - Pearsons & Beniamans
lot

John Watts - pt of Waterford

John Day son of Edwd. - pt of
Maxwells Conclusion, Compd. Rent;
Gay Meadows

Kent Mitchell - pt of the division

William Willson Junr - pt of bush
Grove

Henry Willson - pt of Bush Grove

William Willson - Elizabeth purchis;
Coxes hope

James Osburn - pt of Covent Gardin;
Parkers lot; pt of Covint Gardin;
pt of Osburns Addn.

William Osburn - Hollis Nest; pt of
Planters Neglect; Hollis Chance &
Refuse

Samuell Durbin - Cobbs Choice

Jane Patrige - Thomas Adventure; pt
of Good luck; pt of Thomas's
Range; pt of Richardsons

Charles Croxall - Brothers Inheritance; Hammond Strugle; Hammons
purchis; A lot in Baltimore Town;
pt of Buck Rige; Betsys Chance

Robert Collins - Pork hill

Reverent Thos. Craddock - Rich Level;
pt of Addn.; pt of George's
begining; the Spot

Dickn. & John Brown - Longs Worth;
pt of parkers pallis

George Baily - pt of athold; Bailys
Inheritance; The Hopyard

Joshua Hall; Taylors spring; Addn. To
Taylors Spring; A lot in Baltimore
Town; Halls Range; Taylors
Discovery; Small Wood

Simon Denny - pt of Southampton

Vincent Dorsey - Two lots in Joppa

John Chilcoats - pt of Merrymans
Adventure

Joseph Mayo - Two lots in Baltimore
town

John Cromwell son Jno - Cordwinder
Hall; Cromwells Range; pt Crom-
wells park; Maidns Dairy; pt of
Gist Search; pt Shawon hunting
Ground

David Maxwell - Clarks Denmony in
Antrum and Giles & Websters
Discovery; Jones's gift; pt of
Brothers Discovery

William Banister - Roystons Study

Richard Croxall - pt of Bedford
Resurved; Croxels Elboe room; a
lot in Baltimore Town; Garrison
John Willmot - Litchfield Citty; pt
of Rachels Prospect; Arcadia;
Willmots Wells; Tommy & Sallys
Delight
John Crabtree - pt of Turkey forrist
Joseph England - pt of Fox Hall
Patrick Gray - pt of Logdown Addn.
William McCubbin - Maxwells
habitation
William Roberts potap. - Friendship
Joshua Bond - Joshuas Meadows; 1/2
popler Neck
Willm. Wright potapsico - Carters
Choice
Thomas Michel - pt of Gilberts
Outlet; Gilberts Addition
William Goslin Junr - The Long Vally;
Goodwill
Henry Rutter - pt of Jacobs lot;
Halls Neglect; Rutters folly
Thomas Thompson - pt of pearsons
Lodg; pt of Andrews Addition
Andrew Thompson - pt of Pearson Loge;
Thompsons Choice
William Welch - pt of Taylors
Pallace; pt of Welches fancy
Richard Chinworth - pt of Mereymans
Adventure or Long Cradon on the
Hill; Franklins Gift; Honeys
Delight in Emmas Gardn
Rebecca Rollo - pt of Rolls Adventure
William Cockey - pt of Cockeys Trust;
pt of Shelmores; pt of Shelmores
Addition; pt of cockeys Recovery;
pt of Cockeys folly
Edward Brucebanks - pt of Chance;
Plump Point
Moses Galloway - Gallaways
Enlargement; Marys Adventure; The
Wite Oak Thicket; Jones's Chance
William Ramsey - Farmers Delight
Aquila Hall - pt of Aquilas
Inheritance; pt of New Windsor; pt
of Daniels Neglect; Aquilas
Inheritance
John Renshaw - pt of Giles & Webstors
Discovery; Renshaws Delight
John Hyde of London - Prices
Encoragement; pt of United friend-
ship; Darnals Camp; Affinity; pt
of the Grove; Darnals Sylvania;
Dunkels
Phill Smith heirs - pt of Stout
St. Pauls parish - pt of Enlargment
St. Thomas' Parish - pt of Adventure
Benja. Hammond - Mountain
Eliah Beek [Beck] - pt of Rolinsons
Chance & hog Neck
John Hendrickson - Thoas's Resurvd'd
purchis; Josephs prevelege
Lawrence Clark - John & Isaacs lot;
The Addition
Edward Norwood - Norwoods Chance; pt
of partnership; pt of Batchelors
fear; Benetts Range; Balls Addn.;
pt of Dear Bit; pt of Thomas's
Range; Addn. to United friendship
Cristopher Topham - Newrochester
Benj. Gayton - Temperence Lot
Samuell Merriman - Merrymans
Adventure; Merryymans Chance
Robert Tives - Tredaways Quarter
Samuel Wheeler - pt of Morgans
Delight
Thomas Downs - laws lot; pt of
Gilberts outlet
Peter Middlecalf - Wills forist
Michll. Huff- Hickory Bottom
Robert Jordon - Jordons Delight
Charles Dorsey - Charles's lot
John Hays - pt of Unkils goodwill
Samuel Macarty - pt of the Discovery;
pt of Robin hoods forrist; pt of
Knavery prevented
David Morgan - pt of Parradice
Robuck Lynch - pt of Lidican; pt of
James's Inheritance; pt of Haine's
Green; pt of poplar rige
Isaac Risteau - the Enlarged lot
William Roberts pipe Creek - The
level Glade
Josias Bowen - Jonsas his outlet;
Kinderton
Peter Robinson - pt of Parkers pallis
Benja. Long - Knight Adventure
Greeniff Howard - pt of Caprico
James Stewart - pt of Greendfields
Dan purchis; pt of Woods Chace; pt
of Knavery prevented; pt of Grave-
ly Bottom; pt of Goldsmiths Test;
pt of Gravily hils; pt of

Benja. Choice; pt of hasons
Choice; pt of Wood Choice
Joshua Woods heirs - pt of
Griendfield Double purchis; pt of
Woods Close; pt of Knavery pre-
vented; pt of Gravely bottom; pt
of Goldsmiths Test; pt of Gravely
hils
John Lynch - pt of Cubb hills
Richard Miller - pt of Brods Improve-
ment
Major Thos. Harwood - The lyon; pt of
hazzard
Richard Garrison - Dispach; Timber
Swamp
John Gardiner - Chery Gardin
James Boreing - the addition
William Hall - pt of Pleasent Meadow;
Halls Range
John Denton - Vilin
James Gallion Junr - No name; pt of
Whitcrest Rige
Edward Evans - pt of Bons Manner
George Brown - pleasent Grove; Browns
Delight
John Myers - pleasent Garden; pt of
Bonds Mannor
Andrew Shriver- Mistake; The Addition
James Brown - Bartons Mount
John Cryder - Mollys Industry
Frederick Cryder - Nabourly Kindness
Joshua Cockey - pt of Cockeys trust;
Ties Delight; pt of helmors Addn.;
pt of helmore; Anthonys Delight;
Cowhill
Cristopher Durbin - Durbins Venture
Robert Owings - Bear Garden
Andrew Hersey [Kersey] - The Golden
Grove
John Counts - pt of Diggs Chance;
Wateroake level; Addn. to water
oak level
Samuel Barkall - pt of Batchelors
Choice
Nichos. Corvens widow - pt of Batche-
lors Choice
Ludwick Shriver - Ludwicks new Mill
Phillup Morninstar - pt of Brotherly
love
Addam Hubbard - pt of Brotherly love
Mathew Smiser - pt of providence
Jacob Hook - pt of providence
Edward Corbin - pt of Comberland

James Maxwell - Fathers last will;
Maxwells Addition; Broutons
Trougble
John Riston - Taylors Mistake
Cristian Kersy - Kersys Mount
Burgis Scott - Stone Rige; Addn. to
Stone Rige
Benja. Taylors heirs - Addition to
Narow bottom
Thomas Harrison, Chas. Coty - pt of
Constant friendship
Joseph Murry - Crumwell Morgans hope
Jacob Stroup - Jacobs lot; Maiors
Choice
James Powers - Johns habitation
Patrick Ruark - pt of the agreement
William Kings heirs - Kings Adventure
Hyde Hoxton heirs - friends Adventure
Edward Fottrol - Sweeds folly;
Welches Addition
Eliza Burgis - Taply Neck
George & John Gale - pt of Chevy
Chace
William Mitchel - pt of Bates
Enlargment
Thomas Bale - pt of Bates Enlargment
John Wicks - Rutledges Venture
Ann Greenall - Greenalls Discovery
Murto McDowell - Bring me home
James Boston - Tanners Yard
Joseph Barrell (Barrett?) - The Fancy
Messrs Stodard & Holliday - pt of
Trumans Acquaintance
Jonathan Scarff - pt Browns Adventure
William Cromwell - Joshuas lot; Gist
Meadow; Elyges folly
Nathan Horner - Williams Rige
John Stubs wido - John sons Island
Mathew Hawkins - Hawkins Fancy
Resurvd.
Thomas Watson - Watsons Trust
Benja. Barnes - Absolums Chance
Abner Baker - Abners Delight
Richard Richards - Richards Chance;
Trancilvania; Hogg Island
Joseph Osbourn - Turkey Cock Hall
Thomas Munay - Hunters Forist
Edmund Bull - Whitecars Chance; Land
of promise
John Molonee - timbers Rige; Ulrick
Whistler; Plemoth (entire entry
lined through)

Michael Rawlins - Chattom
Charles Baker son of John - Charles's Delight
John Baker son of Absolum - Johns park; Bakers Industry
Andrew Dorsey - Dorseys prospect
George Shiply - Shiplys Chance
Richard Carter - Egypt
Thomas Alender - Freemans Mount
John Taylor - Ropers Encrese; Howards Addn.; Loyd & Ludloes lot
George Bradford - Turky hills & Staubury hils
William Mattox - pt of Corgaforgues
James Greenfield - pt of Trumans Acquaintance
Edward Garretson - Fox habrour
Bernard Preston - pt of Mathews Neighbour; pt of Ruff chance
George Ogg Junr- Addition to Georges lot
George Ashman - pt of Counterscarp & Addn. to Do.; pt of Ashmans Delight
Thomas Burchfield - pt of Daniels Neglect
Christopher Sutton - pt of Felms (Fulks?) point
Joseph Sutton - Batchelors Delight
Peter Shults - pt of Dilles Choice
Margret James - pt of Claxens purchis
Edward Day - pt of Taylors Mount; nothing worth; Dixons Chance; Taylors Enlargment; A lot in Baltimore Town
Henry Worril - Timber Grove
William & Thos Holtons heirs - 2/3 Miners Adventure
Joseph Bulkly - pt of hopewell
Lancashire Forge - pt of maidins Bower; Rich point; pt of comby Chance; Bennets prospect
Charles Milhuse - The Rangers forist; pt of Ebenezers park
John Davis son (of) Walter - pt of Salt Peter Rock; pt of Batchelors Meadows; pt of Dentons hope; Middle Junifer
Samll. Durbin Junr - Jacksons purchis
John Thompson - The Cabin fork

Nicholas Orrick - pt of Cromwells park; Orlick Meadows; Rich Neck; Williams lot
William Brown Junr - Mount Pleasant; The webit
Richard Jones - Pleasent Meadow
Benja. Deavour - Deavours Forist
Amon Shiply - Amons Inheritance
Richard Hooker - Hookers Meadow
Thomas Towson - Towsons Inheritance
Harman Husbands - Harmans Addn.
Thomas Sheridine Junr - Kindness; Cromwells addn.; Cromwells Chance
Godfrey Waters - pt of Dallams Self preservation
John Keen - pt of Good Neighbourhood
Edmond Talbot - 2 lots in Baltimore Town; Rosannas Range
John Ridgly - 1 lot in Baltimore Town; pt of Clarkes park; Bonds Meadows Enlarged
John Stump - pt of Durbins Chance; pt of Billys lot
William Johnson Bush River; pt of Bons lot
Capt. James Cawley - pt of Edward Enlargment
Baptist Barber - pt of Stansburys plains
James Bartin - pt of Robins Camp
James Martain - Widows Care
Thomas Johnson D. Creek - pt of Giles & Websters Discovery
John Hatton - Males Affinity; Caswells Venture; Richardsons prospect
Rebecca Spicer - pt of Spicers Inheritance
Benja. Barney - Absolums Camp
Peter Goslin Junr - The Dayly incum
George Ensor - Spring Gardin
Francis Brucebanks - pt of chance
Thomas Coal Junr - prices Goodwill; Thomas lott
Nicholas Gash - pt of Goos harbour
Mary Wate - pt of Meritons lot
Phillip Thomas Esqr. - pt of Clagets forist; Bonds Gratuity
Thomas Bladen, Esqr. - Blathinia Cambia; Carsis forist
Joseph Hill - Hills forist

Thomas Cockey - Gardiner Gardin;
Addn. To Do.; Sewalls hope;
Sewalls Contrivence; The lands
End; Bowdens folly; pt of Jemaca-
mans plague; pt of Royall and
Addn. to Do.; Malinda; Addn. to
Do.
Sarah Hill - Sparrows Nest
Henry Darnall - The land of promise
Daniel Dulany, Esqr. - Low Land
Phillip Darnall - The Convenency; The
Reserve; Rich Level
Doct. Charles Carroll - pt of Rich
Neck; pt of George; Carrols
Island; Neglect; Dellengen;
Prevelidge Enalarged; Onions Boggy
Island; What you please; Wm. &
Elizabeths fancy; Hockory(?) Rige;
Bonds Neighbourhood
Charles Carrol Junior - The Caves;
Leford (Lifford); Welches
adventure; Pleasent Green
William Cole - pt Owings Adventure;
pt Owings Additon
Nathan Hammond - Hammonds pursue
Gidion Lintchcomb - Hollands park
Capt. John Howard - pt of James's
forest; Johns Delight
Thomas Sprigg - Sparrows Addn.;
Prevention; Howe Cater Powel
Charles Perpoint - Cannons lot;
Grimes Choice; Perpoints Adventure
James Paul Heaths heirs - St. George;
pt of Stets Level
Doct. Willi[am] Murry - pt of Hills
Camp
Thomas Lusby - Lusbys Adventure &
Fawns Nest
Samuell Galloway - Tayulors Forist
John Taylors heirs - Belts park
Michl. McNamarra - Pimilico
George Platter, Esqr. - pt of
Jacksons Camp
Capt. Walter Smith - pt of Taskers
Camp
Samuel Chews heirs - Margrets lot
John Inch - Strawberry plains
Samuel Howard - The lucky Adventure
John Hood - John lot; Sallys Chance
William Frisby - New Stadt
William Lux - pt of Grooms Chance
Jonathan Rowlings - Brother love

Roger Boyce, Esqr - Mount James; Bear
Neck; Quinn; pt of Hatchinsons
Neglect
Charles Carroll & Co. - pt of Broads
Improvement; Phillips Burgh;
Gorsuch; Brunswick; Johnsons
Interest; pt of George; pt of
Yates's forbearance; Yates's
Addition; The Enlargment; pt of
Rogers Increse; Morphys pleasures;
Addition; The level Formerly the
... level; Organs Fancy; Constitu-
tion Hills; Wills Chance; pt of
Hammons purchis; pt of Brothers
Inheritance; pt of Browns Adven-
ture; Young lot; Ellis Chance; pt
of Parishes fear; Fox Hall; New
Town; Peace and Good neighbour-
hood; Skeymores Adventure; Parishs
Range; Spring Gardin; Slades Camp;
Newport; Buck Range; Cuckhold
makers pallace; The pavement; pt
of Smiths forist; pt of Yates
forbareance; Cooms's Adventure;
Nicholsons Delight; Yates's
forbareance; Marshes victory;
Orrange; pt of Batchelors fear;
Magan's Ambition; Labyrinth;
Frederick hall Enlargd.; Cannons
delight; Gallaway; The Improve-
ment; Bear Hills; Weavers provi-
dence
Benjan. Tasker, Esq. - pt of parkers
pallis; White Hall; Crawly
Contrivance; Morning Choice;
Addition; Maidens Neighbour; Anns
Lot; Pleasent Vale
Joshua Dorsey - pt of Dear hill
Hance Nelson - Little Worth
Lawrence Todd - pt of Todds forist
Bazill Brook St. Marys - His lord
Ships Gift
John Hall son of John - Smiths Addn.
William Keen - pt of Cristophers
Camp; pt of Solitude
Thomas Raynolds Collo - pt of Clauens
hope
Roger Brook Cal. Coty - pt of Broooks
Cross
Thomas King Cal Coty - pt of Brooks
Cross

Capt. Isaac Johns heirs - pt of
Cristopher camp

Walter Dulany - pt of Vale Jehoso-
phat; No Name; Dulany park
Resurvd.; Dorseys Plains;
Charles's Bounty

Jacob French - pt of Fishing Creek

Phillip Jones - Jones's Contrivence;
St. Johns park; Eagles Nest; The
folly; Jones's Prevention; Jones's
Lot

Amos Garrets heirs - The land of
Goshan; Gillingham; Elferds
fields; pt of Solitude; pt of
shepherds chance; Range

Bazel & Caleb Dorsey for Thos. Todds
heirs - Denton; North point; Old
Road

William Hopkins - pt of Batchelors
Goodluck

John Watkins - Anns Dowry

Samuel Gist - pt of Solitude

John Tye - Broadmead; pt of James's
Meadow

John Jackson - Addition to Jacksons
Chance; Woodly's Range

Saml1. Harris - Friend Ship

Mrs. Ann Greenfield - pt of bear Neck

Avarila Day - Arthurs lot

Peter Welty - pt of Diggs Choice

John Litton - Anns Delight; pt of
Arabia petre

Bryan Philpot - Addsbuds Prospect;
Strafford Town

William Holms - Holms Lott

Edward Dorsey Elk Ridge; Bellrake
thicket

John Elder - Elders puzzel; Elders
plague

Shadrack Williams - Shadracks Last
Shift

John Pyle - Pyles addition

Cristopher Gardner - Gardners Delight

Adam Shiply - Adams gardin

Partrick Montgomery - parmacks
purchis

John Montgomery - Johns purchis

Daniel Cleary - Buck Bottom

Samuel Sewall - Samuels Delight

Richard Mole - Davids Fancy; pt Upton
Court

James More Junr - Cumberland; The
Addn. to Coxes hope

Thomas Ensor - Halmwood

Edward York - pt of Yorks Chance; pt
of Bridewell Dock

John York - pt of Yorks Chance; pt of
Bridwell Dock

Cumberland Co - pt of Rigbys hope

Thomas Davis - Hopewells pt of
Arthurs choice

Ann Fishpaw - pt of the hopyard

George Simmonds - pt of Richard Sons
Outlet

Hannah Starkey - pt of Collinburn

Edmund Stansbury - pt of Franklins
purchis

William Pike - pt of Whitecare Rige

James Dawkins - Crosses lot; Level
Bottom

John Shelmoredine - pt of Mount organ
& Jenkins Addn.; Isingglass Gladd;
pt of Ashmores Delight

Samuell Gott - pt of Gunners Range

Mrs. Catharine North - Phillip
Addition

Edward Cockey - Cockeys Delight

Clemment Mattingly - Hanneford

William Cox - pt of New westwood;
West Beginning

Edward Mattingly - Bonds Beginning;
pt of Bonds Fortune; Frances's
Delight; pt of Good Neighbourhood;
Bonds Choice

Benja. Osborn - pt of Chas Den Brad
Neck (?); pt of St. Martins Lud-
gate; pt of Beadly Resurvd.; pt of
Scotsmans Generosity

Doctr. Ephram Andrews - pt of New
Eastwood

Antil Deaver - pt of Sidgly; pt of
Best Endever

Mich11. Webster - pt of Best Endevor;
pt of Websters Enlargment

John Talbot - pt of Molly & Sallys
Delight

Saml1. Webster - pt of Websters
enlargment; Webster forist; pt of
Howards forist

James Nicholson - Coxes prospect

Robert Johnson - pt Unkils goodwill

Aquila Gilbert - pt of Uncles Goodwill

Col. Thomas Sheridine - Sheridine
bottom; pt of Kingsbury Resurvd.;
Sheridines Serch; pt of Cub hills;
Triptons puzzel; Stony hills; pt
of Selsaid; Sheridines Range;
Murrys Desire; pt of Cargaforgues;
pt of Coles harbour; pt of Mount
anys Neck
John Cross - Crosses park
Thomas Hookers heirs - Batch
Col. Willm. Hammond heirs(?) - The
plains parran; Hamilheath;
Hammonds fortune; Parran Enlarged;
Hammonds Discovery; Caroline
Forist; Two lots in Baltimore
Town; Abners Camp; Hammond Rich
Meadow; Coles Addn.; pt of Buck
Rige
John Kimble - pt of Expectation
William Amos; Claxens purchis;
Planters Rige; Joshuas forist; pt
of Ogg King of Bashan
Ronoldo Monk - Turkey cock hall
John Porter - Ashmores retirement;
Meadow Land
John Allender - pt of Arabia Petre;
pt of Ogg King of Bashan; parsons
outlet & Wethealls addn.
Stephen Roberts - pt of ogg King of
Bathan parsons Outlet & Wethealls
addition
Simon Boom - Idle bought
John Price Junr - prices Glory
Michll. & George Fisher - Tipparary
Doct. James Walker - Batcholers hope
Jacob Cox - Coxes Range
Jacob Shilling - Shellings lot
Thomas Boring - Cuckholds point
Benja. Cross - Laws Range
Christor. Carnan - Brothers Choice; A
lot in Baltimore town; pt of Sha-
wan hunting Ground; pt of Hookers
Chance; pt of Sheridines Grove; pt
of Chevy Chase; pt addn to Sheri-
dines Grove; pt of Calf pasture;
pt of Browns Chance; pt of Addn.
to Green Spring Treverce; pt of
Gists Lime pits; pt of Adventure;
pt of Green Spring Treverce
John Wooden Junr - pt of parishes
Range

Solomon Wooden - pt of Parrishes
Range
Thomas Gorsuch Junr - Loveless
Addition
Nichols. Tempest Rogers - pt addn. to
Batchelors Neck
Samuel Hook - 1 Lot in Baltimore Town
John Rigdon - pt of Jinkins Range
James Billingsly Junr - pt of Jenkins
Range
Peter Myer - pt of Broads Improvement
William Anderson - pt of Bucks park
Joseph Lusby - pt of Druses (Drews)
Enlargment
Mary Ruff - pt of Ruff Chance; pt of
Howards harbour
Henry Ruff - pt of Ruffs Chance
David Rowles - pt of Jone's Adventure
- Moles Care
Samuel Forward - Meadins Medows; pt
Contrivance to Coles Chance; pt St
Omer; Colegates Addition
Nathan Nicholson - Limbrick; pt
Midsummer Hills
John Craton; pt uncles Goodwill
Solomon Brown - pt Samuels Hope
Thomas Walton - Baines(?) Level
Soloman Stoxdall - pt of the Reserve;
Stoxdales Content; pt McClains
hils
Eliah Owings - pt of Howards fancy
Charles Howard - pt of Cornelius &
Marys lot; Howards Adventure
Jemine Jackson - pt Halls Rige
James Whitecre - pt of Birr
Charles Talbot - pt of Thomas Bonds
gift
Dan Buckler Partrige - pt of Thomas's
Adventure; pt of Goodluck; pt of
Thos.'s Range; Balliston
Robert Morgan - pt of Paradice
Edward Corbin Junr - pt of Comberland
William Govane - pt of Friends Dis-
covery; Stones Delight; Locust
Neck
William Denton - James's Begining; pt
of Collins Choice
James Briant - Bryants Chance
William Fell - Liverpool
William Wheeler the younger - bold
Adventure

Samuel Cole - Maslinton; Martins
Addition; Charles's Goodluck
William Cole Junr - Young mans
Adventure
Eliza. Body - pt of Balliston
John Gorsuch - Ensors Chance
John Rhodes - Pleasent hill
Mary Jackson - good Will
Joseph Norris son of Edwd. - pt of
Bartons Mount
Isaac Butterworth - pt of Uncles
Goodwill
Thomas Simmonds - pt of Claxins
purchis
William Murdock Esq. - Adventure
Thomas Veasay - pt of Arabia Petre
Caleb Dorsey - pt of Dorseys Milfrog;
timber Rige
George Lestor - Eadon's Addition; The
Gardin of Edon; Spring Garden
Thomas Johnson pap. - Lodgsdown
Addition; Turners Hall
John Ensor Junr - pt of Broads
Emprovement; pt of Shawwon hunting
Ground; Morrimonce(?) Choice;
Willing
John Forty - Caseboltes Delight
Brice Worthington - Norwoods
Discovery; Ruths lott
Nicholus Worthington - Pedicotes's
Range; Peticotes Addition
Richard & Saml. Hopkins - friends
Discovery
Joseph Galloways heirs - Good will
purchist again
Daniel Carrol - pt of Elinor OCarrol;
Litterlong; pt of Burgis's Camp;
pt of Clenmarilia; pt Vale Jehoso-
phat; pt Thomsons lot; pt of Civil
Adventure
John Worthington - Nathaniel Park;
Welches Cradil
Charles Carrol Esqr. - pt of Elie
Carroll; pt of Letter Lora; pt of
Clinmarilina; pt of Cecils
Adventure; pt of Vale Jehosopha;
pt of Thomsons lot; pt of Burgis's
Camp; Comby Chance; Enigness
Groves; level
Robert Boon - Young Richard; Rockhold
Range
Capt. Nichs. Gassaway - Gassaway
Addn.

James Conaway - Robinsons Addition
Richard Wilmot - The Deep Vally;
Wilmots Mountain; Willmots
Wilderness; Watsons Trust; Bakers
Chance
Edward Chote Junr - Buck Range
Charles Shiply - Long Vally
William Merriman - Marymands Begining
James Dougherty - Bold venture
Edward Wan - Wons Chance
Elizabeth Bankson and John Slamaker;
Staines Discovery
Jacob Bond - 1/2 popler Neck
town
Joseph Ensor - Two lots in Baltimore
Thomas Rigdon - Rock Quarter
Martin Taist - the Close; Spring
Gardin
Edward Ponteny - pt of parishes fear;
pt of parishes Range
John Hook - pt Milford
Edward & John Haw - pt Milford
William Amus Junr - pt of Ogg King of
Bashan
Loyd Buckanon - pt of Selsaid; The
level
Edward Oysler - Long look for (lined
through)
Thomas Randell; pt of Joperday; pt of
Bonds Meadows
John Buck - The Goldenmind
Mis Frances Todd - pt of Shaw Won
hunting ground
William Smith - Jonathan Inheritance
Edward Dorsey son Edwd. - pt of
Bellyake Thicket
William Asque - Hales Discovery;
Knights addn.
James Barton - pt of Robins Camp
(entire entry lined through)
John Evins - Evins Venture
Henry Owings - pt of Long Acre; The
Giliad
Thomas Jerman - pt of Salt Peter
Neck; pt of Batchelors Meadows; pt
of Dentons hope
John Pollard - pt of Brooms Bloom
Abel Chanley - pt of Brooms Bloom
John McCool - pt of Brooms Bloom
John Beaver - pt of Brooms Bloom
Samll. Shiply - pt Greenburys Grove;
Malones Resolution
Mathew Coulter - 1 Lot in Baltimore
Town

PETITIONS

1750 Sep 4/Vestrymen and wardens, St. Thomas Parish, Baltimore County. To Gov. Samuel Ogle. George Ashman and John Hamilton are nominated as inspectors for the warehouse at Baltimore Town. Signed: Thomas Cradock, Peter Bond, Robert Gilcresh, John Ford, Benjamin Bond, Samuel Owings, George Ogg and Stepn. Gill. (From Calendar of Maryland State Papers - The Black Books, p. 96.)

1750 Oct 3/St. John's Parish, Baltimore County. To Gov. Samuel Ogle. As inspectors at Joppa warehouse the old inspectors, George Presbury and Nathan Richardson, together with William Amos, Jr., and Heathcutt Picket, are nominated; for Otterpoint warehouse on Bush River, Capt. William Bradford, Daniel Maccomas, James Carroll and Joshua Bond are recommended, the former two being present inspectors. Signed: Hugh Deans (rector), John Paca, William Dallam, William Savory, Walter Tolley, Richard Willmott, Samuel Smith, Daniel Maccomas, Jr. (From Calendar of Maryland State Papers - The Black Books, p. 101)

1750 Oct 6/St. George's Parish, Baltimore County. Nomination of inspectors. The vestrymen and wardens have chosen the following persons for inspectors at Swan Creek and Rock Run Warehouses: Michael Gilbert, Richard Dallam, James Garretson and Samuel Harris; the vestrymen and wardens are: Andrew Landrum, John Hall, James Osbourne, James Garrison, John Hall, Jr., Samuel Webb, Alexander Hill, John Hanson, Robert Patterson. (From Calendar of Maryland State Papers - The Black Books, p. 101.)

(1753-1769) The Inhabitants of Baltimore County. To Gov. Horatio Sharpe and the Upper and Lower Houses of Assembly. Petition for a tobacco inspection warehouse at Fell's Point instead of at Baltimore Town; enumerate the advantages of the proposed site. Signed: Wm. Worane; John Ensor, Jr.; William Moore; Robert Willmott; Samuel Ball; J. Welsh; John Ensor, Sr.; Daniel Coventry; Daniel Stansbury; Robt. Adair; Jon Willmott; Saml. Young; Benja. Rogers; Joshua Hall; Benja. Griffith; Vachel Worthington; Edwd. Norwood; Wm. Barney, Jr.; John Deaver; William Robinson; Thomas Ellett; Isaac Webster; Charles Baker; Jas. Morison; John French; Benja. Wells; Josias Bowen; Benja. Bowen; Nathn. Bowen; John Gill, Jr.; Thos. Johnson; Moses Barney; Benjamin Bond; Absalom Butler; Richd. Jacks; Solin Wooden; Geo: Risteau; John Pindell; Nicholas Brittan; Benj. Hooker; Wm. Randall; John Wilson; Thos. Sollers; Thos. Ford; Darby Harney; Richd. Hopkins; Brian Phelps; Michl. Webster, Jr.; J. Bond. (From Calendar of Maryland State Papers - The Black Books, p. 109.)

(1754 Jun 24) William Keene, Baltimore County. To Gov. Horatio Sharpe. Petitions for possession of 583 acres, part of a tract of land called Solitude in York County, Pennsylvania; Hugh Ross is in possession and has applied for a warrant to survey it; Ross threatens violence if he is evicted. Names: Thomas Larkins; Christian Guest; Samuel Guest; Sarah Gassaway Keene; Thomas Gassaway; Augustus Brown; Dudley Digges. Archives of Md., XXXI, p. 34-35. (Calendar of Maryland State Papers - The Black Books, p. 116.)

(1755) St. Paul's Parish, Baltimore County. Petition of the rector and
sundry parishioners to Gov. Horatio Sharpe and the Assembly. The
petitioners pray for an Act of the Assembly to repair their church.
Signed: Thomas Chase (rector); T. Stansbury; John Frosher; William Wells;
John Wooden; A. Eaglestone; John Stinchcomb; James Cary; John Ensor, Jr.;
Charles Ridgely, Jr.; Jo(hn) Ridgely; Alexander Lawson; William Rogers;
Valentine Larsch; Samuel Hooks; Jann Stohler; Mickel Denninger; Henry
Hofsteter; Johanness Schley; Caspar Walter; Heinrich Mayer; Conrat Schmid;
Mbry (Mayberry) Helms; Moses Wersler; Mayberry Helms, Jr.; William
Partridge; George Hartman; William Wooden; William Pontany; Job Evans;
Robert Willmott; Nicholas Rogers; John Moale; Andrew Buchanan; John
Stevenson; N. Ruston Gay; --- Coulter (?); W. Barney; John Moore; John
Morgan; Thomas Sollers; Elisha Hall; Edward Lewis; Edward Stevenson, Jr.;
Anthoney Gott; William Askew; James Fendall; Gilbert Crockett; John Driver;
John Conaway; Robuck Lynch; Edmund Talbott; William Sargeant Kittridge;
Henry Green; Joseph Merryman; William Nicholdson; J. Bonfield; George
Pickett; Samuel Messerschmit; Henry Crown; Edward Lewis; Andreas Steiger;
Johnes (Johannes) Paul; Johannes Allgeyer; Caspar Grasmuck; Christoph
Gettelmeier; Daniel Berwilz(?); Christopher Settelmer; Vitus Hertweg; Georg
Michael Harttman; Heinrich Gruntzman; Jacob Bar(?); John Reddell; William
Burk; Solomon Wooden; Edward Lewis (M.). Read and rejected - J. Ross, Clerk
of Upper House of Assembly, March 3, 1755. (Archives of Md., LII, p.
667-668 and Calendar of Maryland State Papers - The Black Books, p. 119-20)

1760 Sep 6/William Cox, Baltimore County. Return for 23 pounds 19 shillings
from the Quakers to aid the sufferers from the Boston fire; receipt of the
sheriff, Robert Boyce, for the money. Signed Robt. Boyce
Subscribers: Joseph Hopkins; William Hopkins; James Crawford; William Cox;
Samuel Hill; Skipwith Coale; William Coale, Jr.; William Coale, Sr.; Sarah
Massey; Grace Wallas; Hannah Richardson; Elizabeth Goner; N. Rigbie;
Johnathan Massy; Samuel Harris; John Wilkinson; Hosier Johns; Nathan Johns;
William Willson; Stephen Jay; John Forwood; James Rigbie; Jacob Giles; John
Wallis; Richard Johns; Johnathan (?) Webster. (From calendar of Maryland
State Papers - The Black Books, p. 159)

From Historical Sketches of St. Paul's Parish in Baltimore County, Maryland
by The Rev. Ethan Allen, Baltimore, 1855.
Bachelors taxed sometime during the period, 1756 to 1762):
Those taxed 300 pounds and over were:
Baltimore Town: Thomas Harrison; Doct. J. Stevenson; John Moale; Edward
Parish; Andrew Buchanan; William Baxter; Daniel Chamber Senr; Thomas Dick;
James Franklin; John Mercer; Jonathan Plowman; Mark Alexander; John Shecle
(Sherle?)
Upper hund(red): McLain Baily; John Welch; John Orreck; James Richards;
Edward Pontany; Jabez Bailey
Lower (hundred): Joseph Taylor; Samuel Bowen; Josias Bowen; Edward Bowen;
Moses Mackubbin; Wm. Wood; Nathl. Williams; John Howe; Thomas Sollers; Jona.
Hanson Jr.; Thomas Jones; Edmund Stansberry; Jonathan Harrison Jr.; Wm.
Patridge; John A. Smith

Those taxed as worth 100 pounds and under 300 pounds:
Lower [Hundred]: Christopher Dukes; Laurence Watson; Chrstr. Strangesh(?);
Edmund Stansberry; William Patridge
Upper [Hundred]: Elijah Owens; Solomon Wooden; John How; John Floyd;
Benjamin Banniker; Samuel Bowen; Edward Bowen; Jabez Bailey; Josias Bowen;
McLain Baily; Samuel Howe; Jonan. Hanson Jr.; William Hadelin; James
Richards; Daniel Stansberry; Richard Stansberry; David Rusk; Doct. David
Stewart.
The French war terminated in 1763 and the Bachelors ceased to be taxed.

Church Wardens and Vestrymen of St. Pauls Parish. v. denotes vestryman;
c.w. denotes church warden.

◊ orge Ashman v. 1692. buried Jan 31
1669. [The writing is fairly
clear. The dates are in obvious
conflict.] From 1693 he was the
presiding Justice of Baltimore
County
John Terry v. 1692. called Capt.
died March 4, 1698.
Francis Watkings. v. 1692. called
Senr. of Back River, he was buried
Apr 9 or 10 1696.
Nicholas Corban v. 1692. called Senr
of Bear Creek, he was buried Dec
31, 1696.
Richard Sampson v. 1692. 1695.
Richard Cromwell v. 1692.1695. Middle
[?¶ R.
John Gar v. (1692), vestry's clerk
John Forney v. 1695
Wm. Wilkenson v., 1695
John Hays v. 1695

--- Records lost for 30 years ---

Thomas Biddeson, v. 1721. B.L. in
Back River lower hund.
John Edger, v. 1721
John Israel, v. 1722, a vistor of the
county school. 1723.
John Orrick, v. 1722, P.L. Patapsco,
Lower Hund.
Joseph Murray, v. 1722
John Dorsey, of Edwd. v. 1722, in
1713, High Sheriff, 1723 a vistor
of the county school - called
Colonel.
Luke Trotten, v. 1722.1723.1724. -
took up lots in Baltimore Town in
1730. PL

James Mose (More?), v. 1722
John Eaglestone, c.w. 1722 through
1728 and 1731. B.L. or PL
Christopher Randall, c.w. 1722
through 1726, 1741 through 1743; a
commissioner in 1742 for St.
Thomas Chapel & register of that
parish 1744.
Richard Owings, v. 1722.23
Thomas Hines, v. 1722, 29.30
Edward Norwood, vestry & clerk 1722
Hugh Jones, v. 1722.23
Tobias Stansbury, v. 1722.23 B.L. or
P.L.
Thomas Sheredine, v. 1722-24, 26-28,
30,31,34-36,40-42; 1723 a visitor
of the county school; 1730 took up
lots in Balt. Town; 1732 presiding
justice of Balt. Co. and Town Commissioner; called Maj.; 1745 delegate to Genr. Assembly; died 1754
John Merryman v. 1723.24.25 - P.L.
John Boering(?) v. 1723.24.25; in
1682 presiding Justice of the
county; bought land in Patapsco
Neck 1679
Henry Butler v. 1723.24.25
William Hamilton v. 1723.24.32.33.34;
purchased land 1710; a visitor of
the county school 1723; Commissioner to lay out Balt. Town - and
Town commissioner 1729; in 1734
called Col. and was the Presiding
Justice of the county 1734; in
1736 high sheriff; in 1742 a commissioner of St. Thomas Chapel
John Cockey v. 1722.23.33-35; 1728
purchased land near the Patapsco;
1732 county Justice & Town commissioner

Edward Norwood vestry clerk 1722

Edward Cooke vestry's clerk 1723.24.25

James Powell v. 1724.25; 1730 took up lots in Balt. Town

Philip Jones v. 1724.25.26.32.33; 1730 county surveyor and took up lots in Balt. town

Thomas Taylor c.w. 1724

William Buckner v. 1725.26.27.28; 1729 a commissioner to lay out Balt. Town; 1730 took up town lots; purchased land in Patapsco Neck 1726

Thomas Stansbury v. 1725.26.27 BL

Richard Gist v. 1726.27.28; c.w. 1731; son of Christopher Gist who lived on the south side of the Patapsco as early as 1682; in 1729 deputy surveyor of the Western Shore and a commissioner to lay out Balt Town; died before 1730

Richard Lenox v. 1726.27 PL

Samuel Merryman v. 1726.27.28

James Rider c.w. 1726

William Barney c.w. 1726.27.28.35

James Moore clerk 1726-1733

Luke Stansbury v. 1727-29 BL

John Bowen v. 1727-29 PL

Charles Ridgely v. 1728-30,36-38; c.w. 1732.35; called Maj.; 1737 delegate to the General Assembly

Buckler Patridge v. 1728.29.30; near Bear Creek; BL

Benjamin Bowen v. 1729.30; c.w. 1732

Lloyd Hanes v. 1729.30.31; c.w. 1737-38; in 1730 he took up town lots

James Roberson c.w. 1729

Jonas Roberson c.w. 1729

William Hammond v. 1730.31; called Col.; probably son of John Hammond who settled north of the Patapsco upon lands which ....(?)... for as early as 1695; he was one of the county Justices

John Moale v. 1730.31; a merchant from Devonshire; owned land and carried on business near the Point; 1728 delegate to Genr. Assembly; died 1740 leaving two sons, John and Richard

George Walker c.w. 1729.35; v. 1736-38; a physician; place near Pennsylvania Avenue called Chatsworth in with his brother Dr. James Walker from Peters head Scotland; 1725 came from A.A. Co to Baltimore Co; 1730 a Town commissioner and took up lots; sold the lot to the Vestry on which St. Pauls Church stood; died 1743

John Risteau c.w. 1739; v. 1742-44; called Capt. 1744 high sheriff

Thomas Todd v. 1731-33; son of Capt. Thomas Todd from Va. who purchased lands at North Point as early as 1664

George Buchanan v. 1731-33, 37-39, 45-47; c.w. 1734.49; a physician; came from Scotland & purchased land as early as 1723; 1729 a commissioner to lay out Balt. Town; died 1750

William Fell v. 1733-35, 40-42; his brother Edward a Quaker; 1730 bought Copus Harbor the point; 1745 a Town Commissioner; died 1746; built in Lancaster Street, house standing in 1822

Robert North c.w. 1735; v. 1738-40; called Capt.; carried freight in the ship Content which he commanded as early as 1723; 1730 took up town lots & built N.W. Balt & Calvert Street; 1732 Town Commissioner; died before Dec 25 1749

Francis Hinckley clerk 1734-37

Richard Gist v. 1734-36; c.w. 1738; Register 1739.40; presiding Justice of the county 1736

Edmund Stevenson c.w. 1734

Nicholas Haile v. 1735-37; commissioner of St. Thomas 1742

Samuel Owings v. 1735-37, 44; in 1744 in St. Thomas Parish; he was a county Justice; 1758 delegate to Genl. Assembly

John Ensor c.w. 1736

Alexander Lawson c.w. 1737; Town Commissioner 1746; died before 1768

John Edwards c.w. 1737

Christopher Gist v. 1737-39, 42-47; 1742 a commissioner of St. Thomas Chapel

John Hedden clerk 1738.39

Joseph Cromwell v. 1739-41, 48-50, 58-60

George Ashman v. 1739-41; lived in St. Thomas Parish & a Vestryman there; 1750 Inspector of Tobacco

John Merryman Jr. c.w. 1739.41; 1765 a Town Commissioner

John Gill c.w. 1739; 1745 one of the 1st Vestry of St. Thomas

Jonathan Hanson c.w. 1740, 47-49

Josephus Murray Jr. c.w. 1740

Edward Fotteral v. 1741; died that year; was from ireland; built the first brick house in Balt. Town with free stone corners

Nathaniel Gist c.w. 1741

James Gardner clerk 1741-49

Nathaniel Stinchcomb v. 1742-44; one of the 1st vestrymen of St. Thomas Parish 1745; died in 1746

John Merryman Senr c.w. 1742.46

John Bailey c.w. 1742

John Merryman Jr. v. 1743-45; c.w. 1748; one of the Committee of Safety 1774

Solomon Hillen v. 1743-45; died 1747. BL

Darby Lux c.w. 1743.49; v. 1744-46, 50; died in 1750; called Capt.; 1733 commanded a ship in the London trade; purchased lot on Light Street where he resided & did much business; 1745 Town Commissioner; 1748 delegate to Genl. Assembly

Job Evans c.w. 1743. PL

Abraham Raven c.w. 1744

Mayberry Helm c.w. 1744.50; v. 1748.49, 51-53

Thomas Hanson c.w. 1745; a merchant from Eng.; 1742 built near the S.E. corner of South & Water Streets; 1745 a Town Commissioner; 1746 made an addition to the Town; 1751 the largest subscriber to improving the Town; Market house built on his ground; 1774 one of the Committee of Safety; died 1782

Oct 14 leaving half his estate to the Rector of St. Pauls

William Lyon c.w. 1745 declined as not qualitifed by a residence of three years; v. 1753-55; a physician; he was a scotch Presbyterian and one of the first in opening the Presbyterian Church in 1762

Charles Ridgely c.w. 1745.65; v. 1750-52, 67; called Capt; 1774 on the Committee of Observation; 1776 one of the framers of the State Constitution; 1786 & after delegate to the General Assembly; died 1798. PL

Lyde Goodwin c.w. 1745

Alexander Lawson v. 1746-48; removed from the parish

Tobias Stansbury v. 1746-48. BL

Nicholas Rogers c.w. 1746.52.56; The owner of a vessel; 1753 lottery manager to build a wharf; 1777 aid to Gen. DeCoudry and afterwards to Gen. De Kalb

Sabburt Sollers v. 1747.48 but excused being superannuated. PL

Thomas Franklin v. 1747, 49-51; 1750 presiding Justice for more than twenty years; 1751 delegate to Genl Assembly; called Capt. BL

John Ridgely c.w. 1747; 1742 high Sheriff; v. 1752.53, 58-60

William Green c.w. 1747

William Lynch v. 1747.48.50, 54-56, 66-68, 72

Abraham Eaglestone v. 1748-50, 54-56

Philip Jones v. 1748-50; called Capt.

George Harriman v. 1748-50. BL

John Stinchcomb v. 1748-50, 54-56; called Capt.

Robert Green v. 1748-50

Patrick Lynch c.w. 1748 PL

William Mackubin v. 1749-51

John Walker, clerk 1749-51

Thomas Boone v. 1751

John Long v. 1751.52

Edmund Talbot c.w. 1751; clerk 1751.52; v. 1764-66

Moses Rutter c.w. 1751 M

William Maclean Register 1751 died

William Rogers v. 1751.52, 56-58;
c.w. 1760; innkeeper corner N.E.
Balt and Calvert Streets; 1753
Lottery manager
N. Ruxton Gay v. 1752-54, 62-64; c.w.
1758; 1754 County Commissioner;
1753 Lottery Commissioners; County
Surveyor
William Lux v. 1752-54, 59-61; c.w.
1762.72; 1753 Lottery Commission-
er; 1774 member of Convention at
Annapolis and one of Committee of
Observation, a County Justice
Lyde Goodwin c.w. 1745. 52; 1783
Surgeon of the independant infan-
try; 1786 lectured on the Theory
and practice of medicine in the
Medical Society; a County Justice
James Cary c.w. 1752
Richard Chase v. 1753.54; declined
being an attorney at law; 1753
Lottery Commissioner
Darby Lux - Register 1753; c.w. 1768;
1774 Committee of Observation
John Moale c.w. 1753.55.67; v.
1761.62.70.71.82.83, 85-88; son of
John; 1753 Lottery Commissioner;
built a house which stood in the
... of St. Peters Ch.; married
Miss North; sketched a view of
Baltimore Town; 1763 Town Commissioner; 1765 delegate to the Genl.
Assembly; 1768 Commissioner for
building Court House; 1773 Trustee
of the Poor; added 18 of land to
the Town; 1774 on the Committee of
Observation; a county Justice;
died 1798 at an advanced age
Mayberry Helm Jr - Regester 1754;
c.w. 1757.60; v. 1772-74, 77,
79-81. M
Thomas Ensor Jr. c.w. 1754
Brian Philpott v. 1754; c.w. 1754.63;
an English merchant lately arrived
in 1750; 1751 County Commissioner;
1753 Lottery Commissioner; 1760
purchased the land between the
Harford Run & Jones Falls, and
built at the N.E. Corner of the
bridge; 1762 laid out the ground
in lots; 1775 held a commission in
Col Smallwood's Regiment

Tobias Stansbury of Tobias v. 1754
John Carnan c.w. 1754; v. 1760.61
Capt. Tobias Stanbury v. 1754 BL
Capt. John Wooden Jr. v. 1754 M
John Frazier v. 1754; had a shipyard
Joseph Bankson v. 1754
William Wells v. 1754-56
Zechanah Mackubin v. 1755-57, 59 PU;
1775 on the Committee of Observa-
tion
Hithe Sollers v. 1755-57 PL
Alexander Lawson c.w. 1755; v. 1763
Clerk of the County Court; on the
Committee of Observation
Nicholas Merryman of Saml. c.w. 1755
Samuel Merryman c.w. 1756
Rd. King Stevenson v. 1756-58
Edward Lewis Jr. - Register 1756-58
Thomas Johnson v. 1757-60; see T.J.
1792.
Edward Bowen v. 1757.58
Charles Croxall v. 1757 PU
Christopher Carnan c.w. 1757
John Moale Jr c.w. 1758
Andrew Buchanan c.w. 1759; v. 1762-
64, 67-69; 1768 commissioner for
building the Courthouse; 1774 one
of the Committee of Observation;
County Justice; 1776 Commander of
the Militia; died 1780
John Ensor Jr. v. 1759-61
John Orrick v. 1760.61

BACHELORS TAXED IN ST. THOMAS' PARISH, 1756-1763

Vestry minutes of St. Thomas held 20 Jul 1756: Batchelors in this Parish above the age of 25 and worth a Hundred pounds and upwards: Thomas Cockey Deye; Benja. Whip worth 300 pounds each; Jeremiah Johnson; Rees Bowen; Willm. Cole; Thos. Harvey; Richard Rawlings; Edwd. Stevenson Junr.; Hugh Crayworth, 100 pounds each.

At a Vestry held the 26th of July 1757: Batchelors in this parish above 25 years old and worth 100 pounds and upwards which are as followeth (viz) Thos. Cockey Deye worth 300 pounds and upwards; Jeremiah Johnson; Rice Bowen; Edward Stevenson Junr; Richard Rawlings; Hugh Craugh & Charles Howard worth 100 pounds and upwards.

At a Vestry held in Tuesday 4th July 1758: Batchelors above the age of 25 years, Viz: Mr. Thomas Cockey Deye and Mr. Saml. Worthington worth 300 pounds and Mr. Jeremh. Johnson; Mr. Rees Bowen; Mr. Richd. Rawlings and Mr. Edwd. Stevenson Junr; Mr. Cha: Howard and Mr. Bole Owings.

At a Vestry held on Tuesday 10th July 1759: Batchelors of this parish of the age of 25 years and upwards and worth 100 pound or upwards Viz: Capt. Thos. Cockey Deye and Mr. Jeremh. Johnson worth 300 pounds each and Mr. Rees Bowen, Mr. Richd. Rawlings, Mr. Bale Owings, Mr. Saml. Owings Junr, Mr. Cha: Howard, Mr. John Daughaday, Mr. Nathan Cromwell, Mr. Richd. Hooker and Mr. Thos. Hooker worth 100 pounds each.

At a Vestry held on Tuesday 8th July 1760. Batchelors of this Parish of the age of 25 years and upwards and worth 100 pounds and upwards. Viz. Capt. Thomas Cockey Deye worth 300 pounds and Mr. Rees Bowen, Mr. Bale Owings, Mr. Saml. Owings Junr., Mr. Cha: Howard, Mr. John Daughaday, Mr. Richd. Hooker, Mr. Thos. Hooker, Mr. Nathl. Stinchcomb, Mr. Walter Boseley, Mr. John Fishpaw, Mr. Willm. Barney, Mr. Suthy. Gott and Mr. Abel Brown Junr. worth 100 pounds each.

At a Vestry held on Tuesday 14 July 1761. Batchelors of this Parish of the age of 25 years and upwards and worth 100 pounds and upwards Viz: Capt. Thomas Cockey Deye, Mr. Nathl. Stinchcomb, Mr. John Daughaday, Mr. Bale Owings, Mr. Saml. Owings Junr, Mr. Edwd. Pontany and Mr. Nathan Cromwell worth 300 pounds each and Mr. Rees Bowen, Mr. Richd. Rollings, Mr. Richd. Hooker, Mr. Walter Boseley, Mr. John Fishpaw, Mr. Willm. Barney Junr, Mr. Antho(n)y Gott, Mr. Abel Brown Junr, Mr. Michael Huff and Mr. Aquila Price worth 100 pounds each...

At a Vesty held on Tuesday 13th July 1762. Batchelors of this parish of the age of 25 years and upwards and worth 100 pounds and upwards, Vizt.: Capt. Thomas Cockey Deye, Mr. Nathaniel Stinchcome, Mr. John Daughaday, Mr. Bale Owings, Mr. Edward Pontany, Mr. Nathan Cromwell, Mr. Rees Bowen worth three hundred pounds each. Mr. Richard Hooker, Mr. Walter Boseley, Mr. Wm. Barney Junr, Mr. Anthony Gott, Mr. Abel Brown Junr, Mr. Aquila Price, Mr. John Fishpaw, Mr. Mordecai Hammond, Mr. Henry Stevenson son of Edward worth 100 pounds each.

At a Vestry held on Tuesday the 12th July 1763. Batchelors of this Parish of the age of 25 years and upward and worth 100 pounds and upwards Viz: Capt.

BACHELORS TAXED IN ST. THOMAS' PARISH, 1756-1763

Thomas Cockey Deye, Mr. Nathl. Stinchcombe, Mr. John Daughaday, Mr. Bale
Owings, Mr. Edwd. Pontaney, Mr. Nathn. Cromwell & Mr. Rees Bowen worth 300
pounds each; Mr. Richard Hooker, Mr. Walter Boseley, Mr. Anthy. Gott, Mr.
Aq: Price; Mr. John Fishpaw, Mr. Mord: Hammond, Mr. Richd. Rollings, Mr.
Saml. Bond son of Peter, Mr. Willm. Harvey Junr., Mr. John Gibbon and Mr.
Thos. Johnson worth 100 pounds each.

BACHELORS TAXED IN ST. GEORGE'S PARISH, 1756-1763

These names were copied by Dr. Richard B. Miller from the vestry proceedings of St. George's Parish. Certain symbols were used by Dr. Miller to
indicate the hundred of residence and whether the bachelor was worth between
100 pounds and 300 pounds or 300 pounds and upwards. A = Spesutia Lower
Hundred; B = Spesutia Upper Hundred; C = Susquehanna Hundred; D = Deer Creek
Hundred; X = worth 300 pounds; and Y = worth 100 pounds.

27 July 1756: James Matthews (A, X), Bennett Neal, William Osborn (A,X),
Luke Griffith, James Kimball (A, X), John Kimball (A, X), George Botts (C,
Y), Wm. Husbands, Jr. (D, X), Henry Ruff (B, X), William Johnson (B, Y),
Sam'l Wallis (D, X), James Armstrong (B, X), Isaac Butterworth, John Peacock
(A, X), Rob't Stokes, Samuel Higgins (or Higginson) (C, Y), Aq. Nellson,
Isaac Webster, Jr. (A, X), Edw. Hormby, John Moulton (C, Y), John Jolly,
John Bennett (A, Y), Sam'l Wells, James Billingsley, Jr. (B, X), Amos
Hollis, (David?) Maxwell of David (D, Y), Garrett Garrettson (A, X), Philip
Gover (*C, X), Robt. M. Gay, Gervis Gilbert, Aquilla Johns, Wm. Jenkins,
Benj. Nellson, John Hanson (D, Y),. John Love (B, Y), Wm. Ashmore, Bennett
Neal (2nd listing), and John Gallion (A, Y).

9 August 1756: Bachelor Certificates given to the following as exempt from
tax imposed by Act of the Assembly: John Kimball, Aquilla Nellson, John
Gallion, and Amos Hollis. William Ashmore had a certificate that he was
married before last Vestry.

27 June 1757: Bachelors above the age of 25 (Dr. Miller states that the 1756
list did not identify by hundred or amount; these designations were from the
1757 list, and any name in the 1756 list not having a designation for residence or value was a name that did not appear in the 1757 list. New names
in the 1757 list: James Lee, Jr. (D, X), John Tolly, forgeman (D, Y), Henry
Waters (A, Y), Michael Webster, Jr· (B, Y).

26 June 1758: New names on the list: Richard Johnson, John Lee Webster of
Isaac, and John Hanson, forgeman.

19 June 1759: New names on the list: Jacob Giles, Jr. (X), Samuel Hill (X),
Joseph Hill (X), John Worthington (Y), Thomas Husbands (X), James Creswell
(Y), and Samuel Wilson (Y).

8 July 1760: List of Bachelors: George Clarke (X), David Clarke (X), Josiah
Lyons, William Wood, Robert Dunn (X), John Cooper (X), Thomas Cooper (X),
Stephen Cooper, John Wilkinson, David Tate (Y), Joseph Brownley (Y), Joseph

BACHELORS TAXED IN ST. GEORGE'S PARISH, 1756-1763

Wilson (Y), Edward Hanson (Y), Francis Billingsley (Y), Richard Keene (Y),
Richard Dallam, Jr. (Y), Robert Brierly of Robert (Y).

1761: List of Bachelors: Moses Hill (X), Nath. Giles (X), Chas. Worthington
(X), Robert Darby, Samuel Perriman (or Penninan?) (Y), James Foster (Y),
William Hill (Y), and William McClure (Y).

13 July 1762: List of Bachelors: Following worth 300 lbs.: William Husbands,
Jr., James Lee, Jr., John Lee Webster, Thos. Husbands, Wm. Wood, Moses Hill,
Wm. McClure, John Peacock, Jas. Billingsley, Jr., John Worthington Geo.
Clarke, John Cooper, Chas. Worthington, Jr., Dr. James Spavold, James
Kimble, Rich. Johns, John Love, David Clark, Thomas Cooper, James Foster,
and James Cresswell. Following were worth 100 lbs.: Samuel Wilson, Jos.
Wilson, Wm. Hill, Ed. Wallis, Samuel Griffith, Francis Billingsley, Nathan
Norton, James Kenneday, Jos. Brownley, Richard Dallam, Jr., and Jacob Allen.

29 June 1763: List of Bachelors: Following worth 300 lbs.: Thos. Rigbie,
John Rigbie, Joseph Hopkins, Jeremiah Sheredine, Josiah Lyon, John Johnston,
Nicholas Cooper, John Husbands, Nath. John Giles, Hosea Johnson, Aquila
Paca, John Hall (son of Col. John Clark), Isaac Kimble(?). Following were
worth 100 lbs.: James Matthews, Samuel Perriman (Penniman?), William Fisher,
Philip Coal (of Wm.), Geo. Daugherty, John Briarly, Samuel Smith, John Burk,
James Cannada, Andrew Willson, John Ruth, and David Hanner.

INDEX

Note that a single name may appear several times on a particular page. In looking up a reference scan the entire referenced page to see if the name appears more than once. Titles have been ignored in the indexing (militia rank, senr, jr, doctor, etc.), except when no first names are given. Common spellings of given names have been used in the index but not in the body of the text. Thus the name Jems in the text will appear as James in the index, Samuell as Samuel, etc. Surnames appear in the index exactly the way they appear in the text.

INDEX

CAPPERE John 23
CARABONE Peater 17
CARBACK Ephraim 44; Hesakiah 45; John
    44, 45; Philip 21; Thomas 45;
    Valentine 21, 63
CARDUE Christopher 6
CARL James 19
CARLILE David 15, 16, 28; Robert 15
CARLISLE David 58
CARNAN Christopher 71, 78; John 78
CARPENDER John 17
CARPENTER John 27
CARR Aquila 20, 31, 58; Seaborn 39;
    Thomas 20, 51; Walter 39; William
    23
CARRIL James 18; Peater 18
CARRINGTON John 6, 9
CARRITON John 2
CARROL Charles 44, 72; Daniel 72;
    James 45, 49
CARROLL Charles 23, 69; Dr. 20; James
    31, 59, 73; John 23; Peter 33, 60;
    Roger 23
CARSEY Thomas 4
CARSON Elizabeth 42; William 42
CARTER Henry 24; Richard 21, 68;
    Samuel 19; Thomas 44; Timothy 19;
    William 24, 25, 53
CARTWELL Edward 9
CARTWRIGHT Maray 45
CARVIL John 61
CARY James 74, 78
CASDROPE John 31
CASEBOLT Thomas 20, 62
CASTROPE John 23
CASWELL Richard 18, 27, 31
CATHREN William 17
CATON Thomas 22
CATRIN Richard 45
CAUSELL Thomas 10
CAUTHERY John 12
CAWDRICK John 51
CAWEN John 53; William 64
CAWINS John 51
CAWLEY James 68
CAWS Samuell 12
CAXAN Prew 31
CAYTON Seth 15
CEELY Emanual 7
CELY Emanuel 4
CEMOSE William P. 16
CEMP John 21

CHADWELL John 5, 8
CHALK John 18, 60
CHAMBER Daniel 74
CHAMBERLIN John 17, 22
CHAMBERS Ann 44; Mrs. 44; William 23
CHAMBLA John 27
CHAMBLER John 27
CHAMLET Samuel 18
CHANCEY George 9, 28
CHANCIE George 14
CHANCY George 2
CHANLEY Abel 72
CHANNEL Ann 45
CHAPMAN Robert 22, 23, 28, 30, 31, 52
CHAPPELL Henry 1
CHARLTON henry 53
CHASE John 1; Richard 78; Thomas 74
CHEW Joseph 63; Samuel 16, 43, 69
CHEYS Arther 45
CHILCOAT John 43
CHILCOATE James 26, 31, 37
CHILCOATS John 65
CHILCOTE John 20
CHILL Thomas 16
CHINEWITH Arther 21; John 21; Richard
    21; William 21
CHINNEWORTH Arthur 30
CHINWORTH Arther 53; John 19, 28;
    Richard 66
CHISHER John 13
CHOATE Edward 30
CHOTE Edward 72
CHRISTIAN John 43
CHUBB John 24
CHURN Wilkes 7; William 8
CHURNE Wilkes 5; William 5
CILBACK Cristen 47
CLAGILL John 25
CLARISTON Edmund 2
CLARK David 81; John 14, 15, 23, 27,
    28, 44, 54, 62, 81; John Hall 81;
    Lawrence 66; Richard 23, 60;
    Robert 13, 16, 18, 35, 50, 53;
    Steptoe 23; William 45, 47
CLARKE David 80; George 80, 81; John
    1, 20
CLASOP Jonathan 31
CLAWSEY John 24
CLEARY Daniel 70
CLEGG Ann 27
CLIFTON George 24
CLINCH Thomas 2, 9

88

CLYNCH Thomas 5
COAL Philip 81; Thomas 68; William 81
COALE Benjamin 42; Dennis 31; George
  27; John 6, 11; Margaret 42;
  Shipwith 11, 31, 74; Thomas 30;
  William 11, 28, 31, 74
COB Daniel 13
COCKEY Coll. 21; Edward 1, 70; John
  20, 28, 37, 75; Joshua 67; Thomas
  64, 69; William 20, 30, 66
COCKRAM Thomas 24
COCKS Christopher 7, 10
COE James 44
COEN John 12, Thomas 12
COFINES Edward 13
COGILL Eleazer 24
COINE William 59
COITLY Thomas 31
COLE Benjamin 25; Charles 43;
  Christian 21; Christopher 52;
  David Garnet 52; Dennis 20; George
  25, 61; John 2, 9; Joseph 43;
  Matthew 43; Richard 21, 52; Samuel
  72; Skepwith 62; Thomas 15, 17,
  21, 28, 52; William 17, 59, 69,
  72, 79
COLEATE Thomas 60
COLEGATE Benjamin 54; John 20, 59
COLEMAN Dunkin 21; Nicholas 22
COLESPEGLE John 14
COLGET Benjamin 17
COLLENS Francs 31
COLLET Moses 16
COLLETT Daniel 40; Moses 40
COLLINS Anne 11; Francis (Fran's) 11;
  Gabriel 18; George 45; Robert 13,
  65; Thomas 33
COLSEY Richard 12
COMBESS Jacob 13; John 13; Ketturah
  13; Martha 13
COMBEST Citturah 31; Jacob 63; John
  7; Thomas 31
COMLESS Thomas 13
COMMINS Nicholas 36
COMWORTH Michael 6
CONAWAY James 72; John 74
CONDRON John 52
CONELLY Michel 21
CONEYWORTH Michael 10
CONGDON Nicholas 2
CONNECAN John 24

CONNOLEY Bridget 40; Henry 40;
  Michael 40
CONSTABLE Henry 10; Robert 22, 31
CONSTANCEY Patrick 20
CONTEE Thomas 44
CONWAY -- 47; Robert 44
COOK Barnet H. 45; Jarry 21; Jeremiah
  13; John 9, 11, 25, 28, 37, 57,
  65; Lawrence 11; Modejcap 17;
  Sarah 13; Thomas 21, 60; William
  30, 44
COOKE Edward 76; James 28, 31; John
  5, 11, 31; Sarah 31; William 15
COOKIN John 17
COOLEY Edward 13, 27
COOPER James 21; John 5, 11, 25, 34,
  57, 80, 81; Nicholas 81; Robert
  24, 45; Samuel 11, 31; Stephen 80;
  Thomas 80, 81
COPAS John 2, 6, 9
COPELAND John 15, 31, 63; William 15,
  28, 31
CORAM Thomas 24
CORBAN Nicholas 75
CORBIN Edward 19, 67, 71; Mick 19;
  Nicholas 1, 2, 5, 9; William 19
CORD Abraham 14, 28, 31; Jacob 14, 59
  Thomas 14, 35
CORDE Thomas 4
CORDU Christopher 10
CORIXEN Isaac 20
CORK Tim 19
CORLCUTT John 22
CORNELIUS Henrich 2; Joseph 27, 30
CORUS Thomas 7
CORVENS Nicholas 67
COSINES Edward 13
COSLEY James 14
COSWELL Richard 29, 31
COTHREL Tabi'a 19
COTTAM George 6
COTTENTON Edward 2
COTTINGTON Edward 6, 9
COTTON William 35
COULEY Thomas 45
COULTER --- 74; Mathew 37, 38, 72
COULTY Edward 17
COUNSELMAN George 44
COUNTS John 67
COURD Thomas 7
COURT Joseph 14

McCUBIN John 47; William 47
McCUBINS Loyd 47
McCULLER John 47
McDANIEL Daniel 22; Hugh 24; James 23
McDERMIT Cathrin 47
McDOWELL Murto 67
McFERSON william 47
McGILL Andrew 29
McKENLY Alexander 57
McKENSEY Gabriel 62
McKIM Alexander 47;John 47
McLANE Hector 1
McLENNON Mathew 47
McLOUD William 32
McMACMAKINS Mr. 48
McMAHEN William 47
McNAMARRA Michaell 69
McQUEEN William 60
McQUIRE Michaell 63
MEAD Edward 15, 27, 29, 50; James 15;
   John 15; Joseph 15
MEADS Benjamin 51
MECLANE Hector 6
MEDCALF John 32, 38
MEDDLEMORE Josias 50
MEED Benjamin 18; William 18
MEKIN Hangos 5
MERCER John 74; Luke 60
MERCHANT Joseph 23; Richard 21
MEREDY Samuel 23
MERHAM(?) Edward 26
MERICAN Dinah 16
MERREMAN Moses 19
MERRIKEN Dinah 29; Charles 2, 6; John
   25; Samuell 66; William 72
MERRIMAN Samuel 25
MERRITT George 7
MERRY Nicholas 78
MERRYMAN Charles 9, 21, 29, 32; John
   32, 52, 75, 77; Joseph 50, 74;
   Moses 64; Samuel 31, 76, 78;
   William 21
MERTIN Luther 47
MERYMAN Richard 12
MESSERSCHMIT Samuel 74
MEZTER Danel 47
MICHEL Thomas 66
MIDDLECALF Peter 66
MIDDLEMORE Dr. 35; Josiah 13; Josias
   16, 32
MIDDLETON Thomas 17
MILDUES John 19; Perthm 19

MILES Evan 4, 7; John 3, 4, 7, 18;
   Thomas 18, 29, 56
MILHAUS Bartholomew 32
MILHUSE Bartholomew 29; Charles 68
MILLARD Richard 5
MILLEN Henry 14
MILLER Ezekiel 23; George 26; Horn;
   Joseph 23, 55; Richard 67; Richard
   B. 34, 80; Robert 11; William 23,
   55
MILLKEYE Bartholomew 28
MILLOS John 33
MILLS Evin 4; John 4
MILNER Richard 1, 9
MINCE Joseph 47
MINCHIN Thomas 2, 9
MINCHING Thomas 6
MINCON Richard 15
MIRRITT George 3
MITCHEL Richard 12, 29, 52; Thomas
   13, 22, 29; William 17, 18, 53, 67
MITCHELL Kent 65; Richard 32; Thomas
   12, 32, 55
MITYKA Daniel 44
MOAL John 50
MOALE James 24; John 22, 28, 32, 38,
   74, 76, 78; Richard 76
MOHAM Edward 26
MOLE Richard 70
MOLINEY Peater 17
MOLONEE John 67
MOLTEN John 12
MONDAY Auther 13; Henry 12, 63
MONGOMERY Thomas 16
MONK Ronoldo 71
MONTGOMERY John 70; Partrick 70;
   Thomas 54
MOODY John 23
MOONE August 1
MOOR William 11
MOORE Edmond 1, 6; Edward 7; James
   27, 32, 35, 76; John 21, 74;
   William 32, 73
MORE Henry 13; James 17, 70, 75; John
   63
MOREDAY Samuel 29
MORES Henry 53
MORGAN Henry 52; David 66; Edward 11;
   George 3, 4, 8; Henry 30, 32; Hugh
   60; James 11; John 3, 22, 58, 74;
   Joseph 65; Robert 71
MORGIN Edward 54

PRELLE John 12
PRESBERRY James 16
PRESBREY George 48
PRESBURY (See also Presberry,
  Presbrey, Presby) George 19, 28,
  32, 48, 54, 73; Joseph 36, 65;
  Marey 48; Thomas 56
PRESBY Marey 48; Perigrine 53
PRESTON Bernard 68; Daniel 13, 60;
  James 12, 16, 32, 52; John 14;
  Prichard 34; Thomas 3, 5, 8, 16
PRIBBLE Thomas 4; John 62
PRIBELL John 29
PRICE Aquila 79, 80; Benjamin 19, 27;
  John 20, 23, 51, 71; Mordeca 19,
  32, 51; Robert 15, 27, 29, 32;
  Stephen 65; Thomas 23; William 47
PRICHARD Hanes 56; James 12; Margaret
  13; Samuel 54; Will, William 3, 4,
  7
Principio Company 61
Principio Iron Works 23
PRISE Thomas 17; William 47
PRITCHARD John Henry 32; Obed. 12;
  Obidiah 32; Olds 13
PRITCHET Obadiah 29
PRITCHETT Samuell 13
PROSER Charles 16
PROSSER Charles 40, 41, 42; Eliza 41,
  42; Elizabeth 40; Mary 40, 41;
  Mathias 3, 4, 7; Sarah 40, 41
PUKET Heathcot 58
PULLEY Launcellot 1
PURCHACE George 32
PURCHASE George 12
PURKS Aquilla, Aquiller 48
PYCRAFT Thomas 12
PYCROFT Thomas 51
PYLE --- 47; John 70

QICK Samuel 14
QUARTERMAN John 52
QUICK Elizabeth 36

RAGAN Daniel 23, 32
RAMSEY Charles 3, 8; John 8; William
  66
RAMSLEY William 17
RANDAL Christopher 29
RANDALL Anne 23; Christopher 25, 30,
  32, 38, 75; John 53; Roger 23, 53;
  Thomas 36; William 73

RANDELL Cristopher 55; Thomas 72
RANSHAW Joseph 57
RATTENBURY John 31, 32
RAVEN Abraham 21, 28, 29, 32, 77;
  Abram 31; Isa(a)c 19, 28, 29, 32;
  Luke 2, 5, 9, 19, 29, 32, 34
RAVIN Isaac 51; Luke 54; Thomas 48
RAWLING John 33; Richard 79
RAWLINGS Aaron 53; Daniel 32, 51;
  John 5, 8; Richard 79; William 25
RAWLINS John 3; Michael 68
RAYMAN William 23
RAYNOLDS Thomas 69
READ James 9
REASTON Edward 31
REAVES William 51
REDDELL John 74
REDMAIN Christopher 14
REED Alexander 22
REESE Soloman 12; William 12
REESTON Edward 37
REEVES Robert 2; Roger 2; William 18
REGAN Daniel 29
REID Upton 48
REISTER David 38
RENCHER Abram 11; John 11; Thomas 11
RENOLDS William 7
RENSHAW Abraham 64; John 29, 66;
  Thomas 29, 64
RESTIAN(?) John 38
RESTON Edward 23
RESTONE John 9
REVE Robert 6
REVES Edward 8; Roger 6, 9; William
  34
REVIN Abraham 56
REYNOLDS William 4
RHOADES Richard 18
RHOADS Richard 32
RHODES Henry 43; John 72; William 43
RHODS Richard 52
RICE James 48; Solomon 4, 7
RICHARDS Edward 53; James 65, 74, 75;
  Richard 67; William 11, 29, 32;
  Zachariah 22
RICHARDSON Hannah 74; John 8;
  Larrance, Lawrence 2, 4, 8, 17,
  52; Mark(e) 3, 4, 7; Nathan 22,
  31, 32, 64, 73; Richard 22, 32;
  Thomas 2, 4, 6, 8, 22, 28, 29, 32,
  59
RICKETS Benjamin 64

INDEX

114

YOSTON Henry 55; Laurance 1
YOUNG --- 49; Alexander 22, 56;
    Anthony 22; Aramenta 14; Jacob 23,
    54; Michael 1, 6, 9; Mr. 18;
    Nathaniel 22; Paul 22; Samuel 73;
    Thomas 11; William 47, 60
YOUSTONE Lawrence 9
YUYN William 47